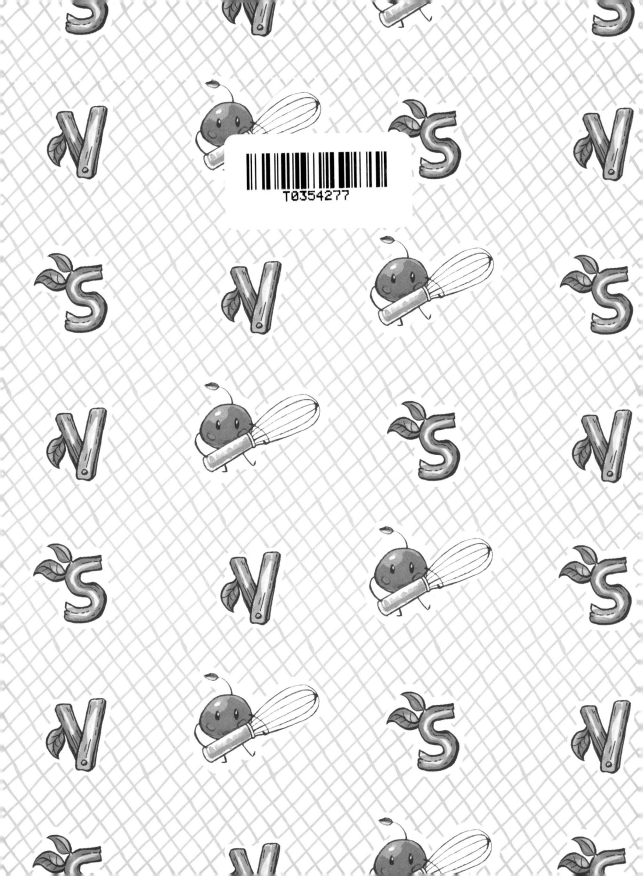

· THE OFFICIAL ·

STARDEW VALLEY

Cookbook

THE OFFICIAL STARDEW VALLEY Cookbook

ConcernedApe & Ryan Novak

RECIPES DEVELOPED BY SUSAN VU

ILLUSTRATIONS BY KARI FRY

RANDOM HOUSE

WORLDS
NEW YORK

Library of Congress Cataloging in Publication Data is
available upon request.

ISBN 978-1-9848-6205-1
Ebook ISBN 978-1-9848-6206-8

Printed in China on acid-free paper

ACQUIRING EDITOR: Kimmy Tejasindhu
PROJECT EDITOR: Matt Belford
MANAGING EDITOR: Chris Tanigawa
PRODUCTION EDITOR: Patricia Shaw
ART DIRECTOR: Ian Dingman
DESIGNER: Laura Palese
ILLUSTRATOR: Kari Fry
PHOTOGRAPHER: Evi Abeler
FOOD STYLIST: Caitlin Haught Brown
PROP STYLIST: Andrea Greco
PRODUCTION MANAGER: Kelli Tokos
RECIPE DEVELOPER: Susan Vu
COPYEDITOR: Carole Berglie
COMPOSITORS: Hannah Hunt and DIX!
PROOFREADER: Janet Renard
INDEXER: Thérèse Shere

9th Printing

First Edition

Contents

My dearest Grandchild,

If you're reading this, then you must've opened my old refrigerator in the farmhouse. Back when I first moved to Stardew Valley, I wasn't much of a chef. However, with all the fresh produce I had at my fingertips, I couldn't help but learn a thing or two about making a great meal. I cooked many tasty dishes in that kitchen, and I know you will, too!

Being a farmer is tough work, but the reward of fresh, quality ingredients at your disposal is well worth it. From farm staples like veggies, fruit, milk, and eggs to wild forage and fresh-caught fish, there's plenty to fill your larder! With the power of cooking, you can combine ingredients to create something greater than the sum of its parts—keeping you energized, happy, and inspired to make the farm the best it's ever been.

Cooking is a special way to connect to nature and other people. What better reason to get your hands dirty than to grow your own parsnips and transform them into something delicious for your friends and family? And speaking of friends, make sure you get to know your neighbors; nearly everyone in town has a recipe or two hidden up their sleeve. I'll never forget that first bite of Lewis's homemade Eggplant Parmesan!

Happy cooking!
Grandpa

ABOUT THIS BOOK · ABOUT THIS BOOK

The recipes in *The Official Stardew Valley Cookbook* are based on the in-game recipes and other foods from version 1.5 of *Stardew Valley.* Though we've tried to remain as true as possible to the original ingredients featured in those recipes, some liberties had to be taken in order to create not only detailed dishes but also dishes that take advantage of more readily available ingredients.

Most of the recipes in the game are simplified for the sake of gameplay; many omit ingredients that are necessary for their real-world counterparts. Then there are a few featuring unusual ingredients that might be challenging to track down. We've gone to great lengths to fill in the blanks and make sensible substitutions where needed, and the end results should speak for themselves. Every recipe has been vetted, tested, approved, and—most important—enjoyed.

Cooking with ingredients that are unique to each season is a fun way to appreciate the distinct flavors that are at their peak for only a short time each year. With that in mind, we've arranged the recipes in this book into Spring, Summer, Fall, and Winter, according to their most prominent ingredients. Whenever possible, we recommend using fresh ingredients directly from the farm or garden. Sometimes that won't be possible because of location, weather, or other circumstances, so canned or frozen ingredients can be used in a pinch. Still, for the best flavor, fresh is always best.

Welcome, friends and fans alike!

It's me, your favorite culinary celebrity, the Queen of Sauce! During my many years as a chef extraordinaire, I've nearly done it all. I've traveled to the farthest reaches of the world in search of the most exquisite flavors. I've mastered the most difficult and mind-bending culinary techniques ever conceived. And, of course, I've hosted my very own smash-hit cooking show on television, where I share some of my favorite recipes from my secret cookbook. But that secret cookbook was little more than pages of scribbles in a binder, not a proper cookbook worthy of the Queen of Sauce name!

So, I finally decided it was time to put together a collection of my favorite recipes from throughout the years. In this book, you'll find some of the most popular recipes ever featured on my weekly show, as well as a selection of viewer favorites from around the world. I've divided them roughly by season, taking into account the ingredients needed and the "feeling" each recipe gives me. There's something for everyone, no matter the season: soups, salads, appetizers, entrées—you name it, it's in here. I made sure to include a little something for dessert in each section, too, along with a tasty seasonal beverage. That way, you'll have plenty of options for weekday meals, family gatherings, parties, or any other special occasion.

If you've been content simply to watch me prepare all these delightful dishes up until now, then I think it's finally time for you to get your hands dirty. After all, half the fun of a home-cooked meal is in the preparation! So, gather your ingredients and preheat your oven; there's a cornucopia of flavors at your fingertips, from every corner of the Gem Sea and beyond!

SPRING

Life returns to the Valley

Spring is a time of new beginnings; the long, dark days of winter begin to recede, and blankets of white snow give way to green as life springs anew. With the advent of warmer weather comes a wide array of fruits, vegetables, herbs, and wild forage. Many folks resolve to eat healthier foods and more natural, homemade meals at the start of the new year, and once the first spring harvest begins, wholesome food options become more and more abundant. Leafy greens, fresh eggs and milk, and earthy veggies provide plenty of opportunities to make dishes that are delicious *AND* nutritious!

These recipes showcase the flavors of spring with crisp salads and vibrant entrées. Are you in search of a delicious, energy-packed breakfast to make harvesting those first spring crops a breeze? Well, then look no further! We've got soft, cheesy, oh-so-scrumptious Omelets and full-course Complete Breakfasts. Need a nutritious lunch to keep you going all the way until 2:00 a.m.? No problem! A bowl of Chowder and a Salad made with hand-picked dandelion greens will hit the spot, I guarantee. Enjoy it with a slice of fresh-baked Rhubarb Pie, and you'll be ready to tackle anything the rest of the day might have in store.

Complete Breakfast

FROM THE KITCHEN OF: **THE QUEEN OF SAUCE**

YIELD: **MAKES 4 SERVINGS**

What do you get when you put fried eggs—sunny side up, of course—next to a side of hash browns and a fluffy stack of hot-off-the-griddle pancakes? The perfect balance of carbs, fats, and protein to give you every advantage when starting your day, that's what! Paired with a glass of milk, a cup of coffee, or another morning beverage, this feast has what it takes to rouse even the biggest sleepyhead. Whether you're looking forward to a long day of harvesting, gathering wood, or exploring the local mines, you'll have all the energy you need to succeed!

INGREDIENTS

Hash Browns

1 pound (450 g) **RUSSET POTATOES**, peeled

2 tablespoons **CORNSTARCH**

1 teaspoon **GRANULATED GARLIC**

½ teaspoon **ONION POWDER**

FRESHLY GROUND BLACK PEPPER

NEUTRAL HIGH-HEAT COOKING OIL, TALLOW, or **LARD,** for shallow-frying

KOSHER SALT

Yogurt Pancakes with Salmonberry-Rhubarb Compote (see Queen's Tip)

8 ounces (225 g) **FRESH RHUBARB**, cut into ½-inch (1.3 cm) pieces (about 2 cups)

¼ cup (50 g) **GRANULATED SUGAR**

3 tablespoons **WATER**

KOSHER SALT

4 ounces (115 g) fresh **SALMONBERRIES OR SMALL BLACKBERRIES** (about 1 cup)

1½ cups (210 g) **ALL-PURPOSE FLOUR**

1 teaspoon **BAKING SODA**

1½ teaspoons **BAKING POWDER**

2 **LARGE EGGS**, at room temperature

2 tablespoons **HONEY**, plus more for drizzling

1¼ cups (300 g) **PLAIN FULL-FAT GOAT'S MILK** or **COW'S MILK YOGURT**, at room temperature

2 tablespoons **UNSALTED BUTTER**

Fried Eggs

2 tablespoons **EXTRA-VIRGIN OLIVE OIL**

1 tablespoon **UNSALTED BUTTER**

8 **LARGE EGGS**

KOSHER SALT and **FRESHLY GROUND BLACK PEPPER**

Hash
Browns

FOR THE HASH BROWNS: Preheat the oven to 200°F (95°C). Fit a rimmed baking sheet with a wire rack.

Grate the potatoes on the large holes of a box grater. Transfer to a large, clean kitchen towel. Gather the corners of the towel, then working over a large bowl, twist and squeeze the potatoes as hard as you can until no more liquid comes out. Set the potato liquid aside for 5 minutes to allow the starch to settle to the bottom of the bowl (it will resemble cornstarch). Pour off the liquid, but leave the thick potato starch at the bottom of the bowl.

Add the shredded potatoes, the cornstarch, granulated garlic, onion powder, and several large grinds of black pepper to the bowl. Mix with your fingers, making sure that the potato starch is evenly mixed with the rest of the ingredients. Set the mixture aside.

Pour enough oil into a large cast-iron skillet to coat the bottom by a scant ⅛ inch (3 mm). Heat the oil over medium to medium-high heat, about 10 minutes; the oil will be hot enough when you sprinkle a small piece of the hash brown mixture into the oil and it sizzles immediately.

Scoop up one-fourth of the potato mixture and drop it into the hot oil. Then use the back of a spoon or spatula to flatten it into an oblong patty that is about ½ inch (1.3 cm) thick. Sprinkle the top of the patty liberally with salt.

Repeat with a second hash brown. Cook both until deeply golden brown on the first side and the shredded potatoes stick together and are easy to flip, about 5 minutes, adjusting the heat if necessary so the potatoes don't brown too quickly or burn. Carefully flip each potato patty and cook on the other side until equally browned and crispy, about 5 additional minutes.

Transfer the hash browns to the wire rack and keep warm in the low oven. Repeat, scooping up 2 more batches of potatoes and flattening, then frying as before. Keep the oven on.

FOR THE COMPOTE: In a medium saucepan over medium heat, combine the rhubarb, sugar, 1 tablespoon of the water, and a pinch of salt. Stir until all the sugar is dissolved and the liquid comes to a simmer, 4 to 6 minutes. Adjusting the heat if necessary, continue to simmer, stirring occasionally, until the rhubarb is very tender and some of it has started to break apart, 5 to 8 additional minutes.

Gently stir the berries into the rhubarb, then transfer the compote to a small bowl to cool slightly while you make the pancakes. (The berries will soften ever so slightly in the residual heat.)

"Grandma knows what's up; she makes me a complete breakfast every morning, which helps me on the gridball field. That's why I'm in such good shape." **-ALEX**

Pancakes

FOR THE PANCAKES: In a large bowl, whisk together the flour, baking soda, baking powder, and ¼ teaspoon salt. In a medium bowl, whisk together the eggs, 2 tablespoons honey, the yogurt, and the remaining 2 tablespoons water until smooth. Pour the wet ingredients into the dry ingredients and whisk until just combined. The batter will be thick and a little lumpy, and that is okay; do not overmix. Rest the batter at room temperature for 15 minutes.

Heat a large cast-iron skillet over medium heat and let it warm for 5 minutes. Cut the butter into 4 equal pieces. When the skillet is hot, add a piece of the butter and swirl to melt and coat the bottom. The butter should sizzle and melt immediately, but should not brown. (If it browns at all, reduce the heat.) Use a ¼ cup (60 ml) measuring cup to scoop out 3 portions of the batter, dropping each into the skillet, one at a time, spacing them evenly apart. Cook until the tops of the pancakes are covered in bubbles, the edges look set, and the undersides are lightly browned, 3 to 5 minutes. (If the pancakes are browning too quickly, reduce the heat to medium-low.) Flip the pancakes and continue cooking until lightly browned on the second side, about 3 additional minutes.

Transfer the pancakes to a large baking sheet and place on the top rack of the warm oven while you make the rest of the pancakes. Repeat 3 more times with the remaining batter, wiping out the skillet after each batch and adding fresh butter, making 12 pancakes total.

FOR THE FRIED EGGS: Wipe out the cast-iron skillet and place it on medium heat. Warm 1 tablespoon of the olive oil until it starts to shimmer, then add ½ tablespoon of the butter. Carefully crack 4 of the eggs into the skillet and cook until the whites are completely set but the yolks are still soft, 3 to 4 minutes. (It is okay if some of the eggs run into each other; you can separate them after they are cooked.) Season the eggs with salt and pepper. Transfer the eggs to a large platter and cover to keep warm. Repeat with the remaining tablespoon olive oil, ½ tablespoon butter, and 4 eggs.

SERVE THE BREAKFAST: For each serving, stack 3 pancakes onto a small serving plate, top with some of the salmonberry-rhubarb compote, and drizzle with some honey. Place 2 fried eggs on a second small serving plate and one patty of hash browns on a third small plate. (Each serving consists of 3 small plates.) Serve the Complete Breakfast with a tall glass of milk, a piping hot cup of coffee, or whatever other morning beverages are your guests' favorites.

Queen's Tip

If salmonberries and/or rhubarb are out of season (or if you simply want to skip making the homemade fruit topping), you can substitute a tart fruit preserve in place of the compote.

Fried Eggs

Farmer's Lunch

OMELET AND ROASTED PARSNIPS WITH BABY ARUGULA

| FROM THE KITCHEN OF: | THE QUEEN OF SAUCE | YIELD: | MAKES 1 SERVING |

I like to think of the omelet as a blank canvas; all it takes is a few eggs and a bit of butter to get things started, and then the sky's the limit! You can add whatever fillings you like, be they veggies, herbs, cheeses—you name it. And what better way is there to showcase the wholesome goodness of farm-fresh eggs than with a sprinkling of deliciously aromatic herbs and Gruyère cheese? By separating the whites from the yolks before beating, we can achieve an airy, fluffy texture that melts in your mouth. Plate it up alongside a batch of Roasted Parsnips with Baby Arugula, and you've got yourself a lunch fit for a farmer! Just be sure to get the parsnips started well ahead of time; they'll take quite a bit longer to cook than the omelet!

INGREDIENTS

3 **LARGE EGGS**

2 teaspoons **WHOLE MILK**

1 tablespoon **UNSALTED BUTTER**

KOSHER SALT and **FRESHLY GROUND BLACK PEPPER**

½ cup grated **GRUYÈRE CHEESE**

2 heaping tablespoons coarsely chopped **FRESH SPRING HERBS** (such as chervil, tarragon, chives, and/or flat-leaf parsley)

ROASTED PARSNIPS WITH BABY ARUGULA (recipe follows)

Special Equipment

One 10-inch **CAST-IRON SKILLET WITH TIGHT-FITTING LID**

RECIPE CONTINUES

Carefully separate the egg whites and egg yolks into two bowls: a large one for the whites and a medium one for the yolks.

Use an electric hand mixer on medium-high speed to whip the egg whites until they triple in size and form medium-stiff peaks, about 2 minutes.

Drizzle the milk over the egg yolks, then use the mixer (no need to clean it) to whip the yolks until the mixture is slightly airy and pale yellow, about 2 minutes. Gently fold the yolks into the whites until just combined.

Heat a medium cast-iron skillet over medium-low heat. Add the butter to the warm skillet and swirl to coat the bottom and up the sides. Carefully pour the egg mixture into the skillet and cook until the bottom of the eggs has set, 6 to 8 minutes. Cover the skillet with a lid and cook until the top has mostly set (eggs should be set around the edges but still slightly wet and foamy on top), 4 to 6 minutes. Season the eggs with salt and pepper, and sprinkle with the cheese. Cover the skillet again and cook until the cheese is melted, about 2 minutes.

Sprinkle the eggs with the herbs. Use a rubber spatula to loosen the sides of the omelet, then fold the omelet over. Switch to a wide metal spatula to carefully transfer the omelet to a plate. Serve immediately, along with a few large spoonfuls of the parsnips.

"An omelet made from eggs laid just this morning, and a plate of parsnip home fries . . . oh, there's nothing better! And it's all thanks to my wonderful brood of hens!" –MARNIE

ROASTED PARSNIPS with BABY ARUGULA

Makes 4 servings

1 pound (450 g) fresh parsnips, trimmed, peeled, and cut into ½-inch (1.3 cm) pieces

2 tablespoons extra-virgin olive oil

2 teaspoons maple syrup

Kosher salt and freshly ground black pepper

1½ cups lightly packed baby arugula

Place a rack in the lowest position in the oven and preheat the oven to 375°F (190°C). Line a baking sheet with parchment paper.

In a large bowl, combine the parsnips, olive oil, maple syrup, and a large pinch of salt and pepper. Spread in an even layer on the baking sheet. Roast the parsnips until they are tender and browned in spots, 35 to 40 minutes, stirring occasionally.

In the bowl used for the parsnips, gently toss the arugula with any residual oil and seasoning. Stir the arugula into the parsnips on the baking sheet and stir gently until some of the arugula starts to wilt.

Transfer the parsnips and arugula to a medium bowl and serve. Any leftovers can be stored in the refrigerator for up to 5 days.

Vegetable Stock

FROM THE KITCHEN OF: THE QUEEN OF SAUCE

YIELD: MAKES ABOUT 2 QUARTS

I'm willing to bet that there are some of you out there who didn't know that you can make a delicious vegetable stock using just about any combination of your favorite veggies. And the best part is that you can use nearly any part of each vegetable to make it—even the parts you'd normally toss! All you need is a bunch of veggie scraps, a pot of water, and some common seasonings—along with a good long simmer, of course. The longer you simmer it, the stronger the flavor will become, so feel free to experiment and taste the stock every now and then until it's perfect. And it freezes well!

INGREDIENTS

3 pounds **VEGETABLE SCRAPS** and/or **TRIMMINGS**, such as tomato skins, corncobs, lemongrass stalk tops, or leek tops (avoid cruciferous vegetables such as broccoli, cauliflower, and/or cabbage, since they will make the stock bitter)

2 **BAY LEAVES**

1 tablespoon **BLACK PEPPERCORNS**

12 cups (3 quarts) **WATER**

In a large stockpot or Dutch oven over medium-high heat, combine the vegetable scraps and/or trimmings, bay leaves, and peppercorns. Pour in the water (or enough to cover the vegetables by 1 inch) and bring to a boil. Reduce to a simmer and skim off any foam that floats to the top of the stock. Simmer, uncovered, for 2 hours.

Strain the vegetable stock into a large bowl and let cool to room temperature. Transfer the stock to food storage containers, cover with tight-fitting lids, and store in the refrigerator for up to 5 days or freeze for up to 3 months.

"In my kitchen, nothing goes to waste! Running the Saloon produces enough veggie scraps to make a big pot of stock once a week. I haven't bought stock from the store in years!" -GUS

Chowder

FROM THE KITCHEN OF: **WILLY**	YIELD: MAKES 6 TO 8 SERVINGS

There's nothing finer on a cold day than digging into a big bowl of piping hot chowder. Those big chunks o' clam and potatoes will help ya find yer sea legs, and the carrots and celery are worth mentioning, too. I tell ya, after a long day of fishing out on the stormy seas, a bowl of chowder's all it takes to warm up me ol' bones once again.

INGREDIENTS

1 large **LEEK**

3 pounds **LITTLENECK CLAMS**, scrubbed

⅓ cup plus 2 tablespoons **ALL-PURPOSE FLOUR**

3½ cups **WATER**

¼ cup (½ stick) **UNSALTED BUTTER**

2 large **CELERY STALKS**, coarsely chopped

2 small **CARROTS**, peeled and coarsely chopped

1 large **FENNEL**, fronds removed (some saved for garnish), cored and coarsely chopped

KOSHER SALT and **FRESHLY GROUND BLACK PEPPER**

¾ cup (6 fl oz) **DRY WHITE WINE**

2 large **RED-SKINNED POTATOES**, cut into ½-inch cubes

1½ cups **WHOLE MILK**

½ cup **HEAVY CREAM**

1 cup **FRESH PEAS** (see Queen's Tip)

1½ teaspoons finely chopped **FRESH TARRAGON LEAVES**

PEA TENDRILS, for topping (optional)

Trim off the tough, dark green top from the leek (reserve or freeze to make Vegetable Stock, page 25, if desired). Quarter the leek lengthwise, then thinly slice crosswise into ⅛-inch pieces. Place the leek in a medium bowl, fill the bowl with cold water, and use your hands to separate the pieces and coax out any remaining dirt. Drain through a fine-mesh strainer and repeat this process until there is no dirt left. Dry the leek pieces well.

Place the clams in a large bowl and fill with enough cold water to cover the top of the clams by 1 inch. Sprinkle 1 tablespoon of the flour over the water and use your hands to stir it into the water and around the clams. Set the clams aside for 15 minutes. The clams will eat the flour and spit it out, which will also help remove any dirt. Drain the water and do this once more with another tablespoon of flour. Rinse the clams well under cold running water.

In a large Dutch oven over medium-high heat, bring the water to a low boil, about 10 minutes. Add the clams, cover with a tight-fitting lid, and cook until the clams open, 5 to 7 minutes; hold the lid firmly and give the pot a good shake several times during the cooking process. Use a slotted spoon to transfer the clams to a large bowl. Strain the cooking liquid through a fine-mesh sieve into another large bowl. Reserve the clams and clam broth.

In the same Dutch oven (no need to clean it) set over medium heat, add the butter and cook just until melted. Add the celery, carrots, leek, and fennel. Season with salt and pepper, and cook, stirring occasionally, until all the vegetables are softened except the carrots (they will still be crisp-tender at this point), about 15 minutes. Add the wine and cook, stirring frequently, until it is almost gone, 5 to 7 minutes. Add the remaining ⅓ cup flour and cook, stirring constantly, for 3 minutes. Stir in half the reserved clam broth until smooth, then add the remaining clam broth and stir again until there are no visible clumps of flour. Add the potatoes and simmer, stirring occasionally, until the potatoes are tender and the soup has thickened to the consistency of gravy, 22 to 25 minutes.

Meanwhile, remove the clams from their shells and roughly chop them; discard the shells. Reduce the heat in the Dutch oven to medium and stir in the milk and cream, then sprinkle in the peas and cook until the milk mixture is hot and steamy and the peas are bright green and tender, 5 to 7 minutes. Stir in the chopped clams and the tarragon, and cook until the clams are hot, 2 to 3 minutes more. Taste the chowder and season with salt and pepper. Ladle the soup into bowls and top with a sprinkle of hand-torn pieces of the fennel fronds and the pea tendrils, if using. Serve immediately.

"I wonder if frogs eat clams . . ." -SEBASTIAN

Fiddlehead Risotto

FROM THE KITCHEN OF: THE QUEEN OF SAUCE

YIELD: MAKES 4 TO 6 SERVINGS

The fiddlehead fern is one of the more unique culinary delights I've encountered. At their peak for mere days each year, fiddleheads are young fern fronds that haven't yet begun to unfurl. They're a prized ingredient in cuisines the world over, and have been enjoyed for longer than anyone can seem to remember. Traditionally, simple preparations are used to allow their deep forest flavor to shine through.

We'll be boiling our fiddleheads briefly first to help break down some less savory compounds and to maintain a nice bright green color, and then we'll give them a final sauté as our risotto is finishing up. Risotto can be a bit hands-on as rice dishes go, but there's no need to worry; as long as you keep the heat steady and add the vegetable stock gradually, you'll do just fine. I believe in you!

INGREDIENTS

12 ounces **FRESH FIDDLEHEAD FERNS** (see Queen's Tip)

KOSHER SALT

6 cups **VEGETABLE STOCK** (page 25)

3 tablespoons **EXTRA-VIRGIN OLIVE OIL**, plus more as needed

1 large **SHALLOT**, finely diced

FRESHLY GROUND BLACK PEPPER

4 **GARLIC CLOVES**, minced

2 cups **ARBORIO RICE**

¾ cup (6 fl oz) **DRY WHITE WINE**

½ cup freshly grated **PECORINO CHEESE**, plus more for serving

3 tablespoons **UNSALTED BUTTER**

2 tablespoons coarsely chopped **FRESH FLAT-LEAF PARSLEY**

1 tablespoon lightly packed grated **FRESH LEMON ZEST**

Hand-torn **FRESH CHERVIL LEAVES**, for garnish

"I usually order the Big n' Cheesy from Gus's, but I saw Emily eating a bowl of this risotto the other day, so I'm trying to develop a taste for the stuff. Don't tell anyone!" –CLINT

Queen's Tip

Instead of fiddlehead ferns, you can substitute 1 pound medium asparagus (about 1 bunch) to top the risotto. Trim the woody ends, then cut the asparagus into 1- to 1½-inch pieces. Reduce the cooking time in the boiling water to 30 seconds and the sautéing time to 2 to 3 minutes.

Fill a large saucepan with water and bring to a boil over medium-high heat. Meanwhile, remove any papery covering from the fiddlehead ferns and wash the fiddleheads well under cold running water. Fill a medium bowl with ice water, season the water aggressively with salt, and set aside. Line a large plate with paper towels.

Once the water is at a boil, season it aggressively with salt, then add the fiddleheads. Cook, stirring occasionally, until the fiddleheads turn bright green and are crisp-tender, 5 to 7 minutes. Use a slotted spoon to transfer the fiddleheads to the ice bath. Stir several times until the fiddleheads are no longer hot, then transfer to the paper-towel-lined plate and set aside.

In a medium saucepan over medium-high heat, bring the stock to a low boil, then cover and reduce the heat to low.

In a large high-sided skillet over medium heat, warm 2 tablespoons of the olive oil. Add the shallot, season with salt and pepper, and cook, stirring occasionally, until softened, 6 to 8 minutes. Add the garlic and cook, stirring constantly, until softened, about 2 minutes.

Increase the heat slightly, stir in the rice, and cook, stirring frequently, until the rice is lightly toasted and smells nutty, 3 to 5 minutes. Pour

in the wine and simmer, stirring occasionally, until most of the wine has been absorbed, about 2 minutes.

Add 1 cup of the hot stock and cook, stirring constantly, until the stock is absorbed by the rice, 3 to 4 minutes. Repeat with a second cup of stock. Continue adding stock, now only a ½ cup at a time, stirring and cooking until the rice is just tender, about 25 minutes total cooking time. Adjust the heat as needed during the cooking process to maintain an active simmer. (You may not use all the stock; save any remaining to loosen the risotto later, if needed.)

Reduce the heat to low, add the pecorino and 2 tablespoons of the butter, and stir vigorously until the rice is creamy, about 1 minute. Remove from the heat, season to taste with salt and pepper, and cover with a lid to keep warm.

In a large cast-iron skillet set on medium heat, warm the remaining tablespoon olive oil. Add the remaining tablespoon butter and swirl the skillet until melted. Add the fiddleheads and season liberally with salt and pepper. Cook, stirring occasionally, until tender and hot throughout, 3 to 4 minutes. Remove from the heat and stir in the parsley and lemon zest.

To serve, spoon the hot risotto (if it thickens slightly as it sits, stir in a large splash of stock to make it creamy again) into 4 to 6 large serving bowls and top with the sautéed fiddleheads. Drizzle with more olive oil, sprinkle with additional pecorino cheese, and garnish with the chervil. Serve immediately.

Fiddlehead
Risotto
28

Pizza
32

Pizza

WITH FRESH SPRING TOPPINGS AND A CAULIFLOWER CRUST OPTION

FROM THE KITCHEN OF:	THE QUEEN OF SAUCE

YIELD: **MAKES 2 (11½-inch; 29 cm) PIZZAS; each serves 3 or 4**

Pizza is almost more of a concept than a recipe; once you've got yourself a proper crust ready for sauce and toppings, the world is your oyster—and yes, you can absolutely top a pizza with oysters! We tackle two different types of crust here: a traditional risen dough made with all-purpose flour, and a flourless crust made with cauliflower. We also explore two different topping styles, including one with a tomato sauce and the other with an olive oil base. By the time you're done, you'll have all the knowledge you need to make the pizza of your dreams. Oh, and if you have a favorite canned or jarred sauce, go right ahead and use it; it's your pizza, after all!

INGREDIENTS

Standard Pizza Crust

1⅓ cups (315 ml) lukewarm **WATER**

2 teaspoons **GRANULATED SUGAR**

1 (¼ oz; 7 g) packet **ACTIVE DRY YEAST**

5 tablespoons (75 ml) **EXTRA-VIRGIN OLIVE OIL**

2½ cups (350 g) **ALL-PURPOSE FLOUR**, plus more for dusting

1 cup (140 g) **WHOLE WHEAT FLOUR**

2 teaspoons **KOSHER SALT**

¼ cup (25 g) grated **PARMESAN CHEESE**

Spring Greens Pizza with Tomato Sauce

2 large, ripe **PLUM TOMATOES**

2 tablespoons plus
2 teaspoons **EXTRA-VIRGIN
OLIVE OIL**

1 **GARLIC CLOVE**, minced

Pinch of **GRANULATED
SUGAR**

¼ teaspoon **DRIED OREGANO**

Pinch of **RED PEPPER FLAKES**

KOSHER SALT

½ cup (40 g) thinly sliced
FRESH FENNEL, plus
chopped **FENNEL FRONDS**
for garnish

¼ cup (25 g) thinly sliced
SCALLION WHITES, plus
2 tablespoons thinly sliced
GREENS for garnish

½ cup (50 g) **FRESH SUGAR
SNAP PEAS**, trimmed and cut
in half on bias

**FRESHLY GROUND BLACK
PEPPER**

¾ cup (75 g) shredded
**WHOLE MILK LOW-MOISTURE
MOZZARELLA CHEESE**

1 tablespoon grated
PARMESAN CHEESE

Asparagus, Mushroom, and Goat Cheese Pizza

6 fresh medium **ASPARAGUS
SPEARS**, sliced on bias into
1-inch (2.5 cm) pieces

2 ounces (55 g) **FRESH WILD
MUSHROOMS**, such as oyster
or chanterelles, hand-torn
into large pieces

1 tablespoon plus
2 teaspoons **EXTRA-VIRGIN
OLIVE OIL**

KOSHER SALT and **FRESHLY
GROUND BLACK PEPPER**

¾ cup (75 g) shredded
**WHOLE MILK LOW-MOISTURE
MOZZARELLA CHEESE**

1 tablespoon grated
PARMESAN CHEESE

2 ounces (55 g) **GOAT
CHEESE (CHÈVRE)**, at room
temperature

2 tablespoons **HEAVY CREAM**

1 tablespoon thinly sliced
FRESH CHIVES

> "Last night I accidentally dribbled marinara sauce all over Sebastian's copy of *Solarion Chronicles*. . . . Maybe next time I'll order a normal pizza instead of the 'wet n' saucy'!" -SAM

MAKE THE PIZZA DOUGH: In a medium bowl, whisk together the water and sugar. Sprinkle the yeast on top, then let sit until foamy, about 10 minutes. Stir in 3 tablespoons of the olive oil.

In a large bowl, whisk together the all-purpose flour, whole wheat flour, and salt. Make a well in the center and pour in the yeast mixture. Gradually stir with a rubber spatula or wooden spoon until a rough dough forms. Sprinkle the Parmesan cheese on top and stir until combined (the dough will still be quite shaggy at this point).

Lightly flour a work surface and turn out the dough onto it. Knead the dough until it is smooth and elastic, about 5 minutes, dusting with more flour, if needed. Cut the dough in half, then roll each half into a ball. Brush 2 large bowls each with 1 tablespoon of the remaining olive oil, add a dough ball to each, and turn to coat well with the oil. Cover the bowls and set aside at room temperature until they are doubled in size, about 1½ hours.

BEGIN THE TOMATO SAUCE TOPPING: Cut each plum tomato in half. Put a box grater into a shallow bowl and grate the cut sides of the tomatoes on the large holes. The grated flesh of the tomato will fall into the bowl, and you will be left with just the tomato skins (which you can save to make Vegetable Stock, page 25).

In a small saucepan over medium heat, add 1 tablespoon of the olive oil and the garlic. Cook, stirring constantly, until the garlic is softened, 1 to 2 minutes. Add the grated tomatoes, sugar, oregano, red pepper flakes, and a big pinch of salt. Bring to a simmer and cook, stirring occasionally, until most of the tomato juice has evaporated and the sauce has thickened, about 10 minutes. Remove from the heat and let cool at room temperature.

In a medium bowl, combine the fennel, scallion whites, sugar snap peas, and remaining 2 teaspoons olive oil. Season with salt and pepper, and toss to combine.

BEGIN THE ASPARAGUS, MUSHROOM, AND GOAT CHEESE TOPPING: In a medium bowl, combine the asparagus, mushrooms, and 2 teaspoons of olive oil. Season with salt and pepper, and toss to combine.

About 30 minutes before you are ready to bake the pizzas, put a large pizza stone or an inverted rimmed baking sheet on the lowest oven rack and preheat the oven to 475°F (245°C).

ASSEMBLE THE TOMATO SAUCE PIZZA: Place a large piece of parchment paper on your work surface. Place a dough ball in the center of the paper and use your hands to stretch and press the dough into an 11½-inch (29 cm) round. As you stretch the dough, use your fingers to press the dough so that it is thinner in the center, with a thicker ½-inch (1.3 cm) border. (This thicker border will form the crust while the thinner center portion will ensure the dough becomes crispy in the oven.) Brush the dough all over with 1 tablespoon of the olive oil. Spread the tomato sauce from the center of the dough outward, then scatter the mozzarella on top of the sauce and sprinkle with the Parmesan cheese. Scatter the vegetable mixture evenly on top of the cheese.

BAKE THE PIZZA: Transfer the pizza (using the paper) onto an inverted large baking sheet, then slide the pizza (with the paper) onto the hot pizza stone or inverted baking sheet in the oven. Bake until the crust is puffed and deeply golden brown, and the cheese is melted and lightly browned in spots, 12 to 15 minutes.

Let the pizza cool for a couple of minutes. Sprinkle with the scallion greens and fennel fronds. Cut into wedges and serve immediately.

ASSEMBLE THE ASPARAGUS, MUSHROOM, AND GOAT CHEESE PIZZA: Place the second dough ball in the center of another piece of parchment paper and stretch and press the dough as you did for the first pizza. Brush the dough all over with 1 tablespoon of the olive oil. Scatter the mozzarella cheese from the center outward, then sprinkle with the Parmesan cheese. Scatter the asparagus mixture on top of the cheese.

BAKE THE PIZZA: Transfer the pizza (using the paper) onto an inverted large baking sheet, then slide the pizza (with the paper) onto the hot pizza stone or inverted baking sheet in the oven. Bake until the crust is puffed and deeply golden brown, and the cheese is melted and lightly browned in spots, 12 to 15 minutes.

While the asparagus, mushroom, and goat cheese pizza is baking, combine the goat cheese, cream, and a couple large grindings of black pepper in a small bowl. Whisk until smooth and lightly fluffy. Stir in the chives.

Dollop the hot asparagus, mushroom, and goat cheese pizza with the whipped cheese and cream topping, then let it cool for a couple of minutes. Cut into wedges and serve immediately.

CAULIFLOWER PIZZA CRUST

Makes 1 (11-inch; 28 cm) crust

Extra-virgin olive oil

1 medium (1½ pounds; 675 g) cauliflower

1 large egg

1 large egg white

½ cup (50 g) shredded whole-milk mozzarella cheese

3 tablespoons grated Parmesan cheese

Kosher salt

SPECIAL EQUIPMENT: Steamer basket and pot

Put a large pizza stone or an inverted rimmed baking sheet on the lowest rack of the oven and preheat the oven to 400°F (200°C). Line a medium baking sheet with parchment paper, then lightly grease the paper with a thin layer of olive oil.

Trim the leaves from the cauliflower and remove the core. Cut the cauliflower into small florets, about 1 inch (2.5 cm), small enough to fit easily in the bowl of a food processor. Place the florets in the processor and pulse until very finely chopped, about 3 cups (1 pound).

Fill a large pot with 2 inches (5 cm) of water, then cover with a tight-fitting lid and bring to a boil over medium-high heat. Cut a large double-layer of cheesecloth, wet it under cold water, squeeze out the excess water, then drape it inside a large steamer insert.

Spread the cauliflower on the cheesecloth in an even layer. Fold any excess cheesecloth over the cauliflower, then put the steamer insert with the cauliflower into the pot. Cover again with the lid and steam until the cauliflower is crisp-tender, about 5 minutes. Lift the strainer from the pot and place it on a baking sheet or kitchen towel to catch excess water. Let cool completely.

Place the cheesecloth-wrapped cauliflower in the center of a clean kitchen towel. Gathering up the towel and cheesecloth together, wring out all liquid. (This step is extremely important because the moisture can make the crust soggy.)

In a large bowl, whisk together the egg and egg white. Add the riced cauliflower, the mozzarella and Parmesan cheeses, and ½ teaspoon salt. Stir until well combined, then turn out onto the center of the prepared baking sheet. Use your hands to spread the mixture evenly to an 11-inch (28 cm) round pizza crust. Brush all over with some olive oil. Place the baking sheet on the hot pizza stone or inverted baking sheet and bake until the top of the crust is set, completely dry, and golden brown in spots, about 25 minutes. You should be able to lift up a corner of the crust and it should hold together.

Remove the baking sheet from the oven and increase the oven temperature to 450°F (230°C).

Top the baked crust with sauce (if any) and toppings of your choice, return it to the oven, and bake until the edges of the crust are deep golden brown and crispy, about 15 minutes.

Let the pizza cool for 5 minutes, then cut into wedges and serve.

Carp Surprise

CARP BAKED WITH SPRING VEGETABLES

FROM THE KITCHEN OF: **THE QUEEN OF SAUCE**

YIELD: **MAKES 4 SERVINGS**

Hey, ever have a bunch of carp lying around and no idea what to do with them? Yeah, me too. Well, I've devised a great solution to this all-too-common problem. I call it . . . Carp Surprise!

This carp-centric dish is sure to please even the most discerning palate. Lightly seasoned fish fillets are individually bundled up in parchment paper along with an assortment of fresh vegetables and baked to perfection, allowing a myriad of tastes and aromas to mingle and evolve. Each bundle is practically bursting with the delectable flavors of spring, full of delicious veggies and moist, tender carp. Who said simple, all-in-one meals couldn't be tasty?

INGREDIENTS

1 large **LEEK**

1 medium **FENNEL BULB**, fronds trimmed, bulb cored and thinly sliced

4 large **RAINBOW SWISS CHARD LEAVES**, stems thinly sliced and leaves hand-torn into large bite-size pieces

¾ cup **FRESH PEAS**

3 **GARLIC CLOVES**, thinly sliced

2 tablespoons plus 2 teaspoons **EXTRA-VIRGIN OLIVE OIL**

⅓ cup hand-torn **FRESH CHERVIL LEAVES** with soft stems

KOSHER SALT and **FRESHLY GROUND BLACK PEPPER**

4 (5–6 oz) skinless **CARP FILLETS** or **OTHER FRESHWATER FISH**

½ cup (4 fl oz) **DRY WHITE WINE**

2 tablespoons **CAPERS**, drained

1 (3-tablespoon) chunk of **UNSALTED BUTTER**, cut into 8 thin pats

1 small **LEMON**, trimmed and cut into 4 thin slices

"This dish reminds me of something me ol' Pappy used to say: 'Don't judge a fish by its fervor, judge it by its flavor.' Even the easiest fish to catch can make a tasty meal!" –WILLY

Position 2 racks in the upper and lower thirds of the oven and preheat the oven to 425°F.

Fold four 12 x 16-inch pieces of parchment paper in half crosswise and trim the corners of each to cut out a large heart shape. (The shape does not have to be perfect, and it is better to err on the side of too large than to cut off too much paper.) Unfold the sheets and arrange the hearts on the baking sheets.

Trim the tough green top from the leek (reserve or freeze to make Vegetable Stock, page 25, if desired), then quarter the leek lengthwise. Cut each piece into ⅛-inch slices. Place the leek in a medium bowl, fill the bowl with cold water, and use your hands to separate the pieces and coax out any remaining dirt. Drain in a fine-mesh strainer. Spread the leek out on a towel and dry well.

In a large bowl, combine the leek, fennel, chard, peas, and garlic. Drizzle with 2 tablespoons of the olive oil, then season with salt and pepper. Use your hands to rub the oil and seasoning into the vegetables; the vegetables should wilt slightly. Mix in the chervil.

Evenly divide the vegetables among the parchment hearts, keeping the vegetables on the right side of the shape. Brush the fish fillets all over with the remaining 2 teaspoons olive oil and season with salt and pepper. Place a fillet on top of each pile of vegetables. Evenly drizzle the wine over the fish and vegetables, and sprinkle with the capers. Place 2 pats of butter on each fish, and top each with a lemon slice.

Fold the top half of the heart over the fish and vegetables, then use your fingers to make small overlapping folds along the edges of the parchment to seal the packets. As you fold the parchment, make sure to press and pinch together the paper edges to ensure that steam will not escape during the cooking (tie loosely with string, if desired). Place the sheet

with the packets in the oven and bake until the parchment paper puffs up slightly and is lightly browned in spots, about 15 minutes.

Transfer the packets to 4 large dinner plates. Being very careful to avoid the hot steam arising, unfold the edges of the parchment hearts or use kitchen shears to cut the packets open through the top. Serve immediately.

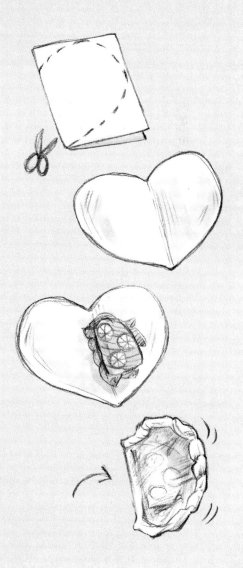

Carp
Surprise
36

Stir Fry
40

Stir Fry

FROM THE KITCHEN OF: **THE QUEEN OF SAUCE**

YIELD: **MAKES 4 SERVINGS**

Unlock the aromas of your favorite veggies with a generous application of heat and just a bit of oil. Feel free to get creative, subbing in different vegetables depending on the season. Once you've mastered the technique, there's no limit to what you can do! If you have a wok available, that's the ideal cooking vessel, but any large skillet will do in a pinch. The most important piece of advice I can give is to keep everything moving; nothing's worse than a burnt ingredient or two throwing off all the other wonderful flavors. I mean, that's why they call it a stir fry!

INGREDIENTS

¼ cup **VEGETABLE STOCK** (page 25)

2 tablespoons **SOY SAUCE**, plus more as desired

1 tablespoon **RICE WINE VINEGAR**

1 tablespoon **TOASTED SESAME OIL**

½ teaspoon **GRANULATED SUGAR**

Pinch of **GROUND WHITE PEPPER**

2 teaspoons **CORNSTARCH**

2 tablespoons neutral high-heat **COOKING OIL, TALLOW,** or **LARD,** for frying

12 large **FRESH SHIITAKE MUSHROOMS,** stemmed, caps cut in half

2 small **PURPLE CARROTS,** thinly sliced diagonally

1 small **YELLOW ONION,** thinly sliced

1 (1-inch) piece **FRESH GINGER,** peeled and sliced into short, thin matchsticks

3 **GARLIC CLOVES,** minced

4 ounces **SNOW PEAS,** trimmed

1 bunch **TUSCAN KALE,** stemmed and hand-torn into large bite-size pieces

TOASTED SESAME SEEDS, for garnish

STEAMED RICE, hot, for serving

Give the sauce a good stir, then pour it over the vegetables. Bring to a boil and cook, stirring constantly, until the sauce thickens to a glaze that coats the vegetables, about 1 minute. Remove from the heat and serve the stir-fry immediately, garnished with the toasted sesame seeds. Serve the rice alongside.

In a small bowl, whisk together the stock, soy sauce, vinegar, sesame oil, sugar, and white pepper. Add the cornstarch and whisk again until the cornstarch is completely dissolved.

Heat a large wok or very large cast-iron skillet over medium-high heat. Add the cooking oil and swirl to coat the bottom. When the oil starts to shimmer and lightly smoke, add the mushrooms and stir-fry until lightly browned around the edges and starting to soften, 2 to 3 minutes. Scatter the carrots and onion over the mushrooms and stir-fry until just starting to become crisp-tender, 3 to 4 minutes. Add the ginger and garlic and stir-fry until slightly softened and aromatic, about 30 seconds. Add the snow peas and kale, then add a large splash of water and stir-fry until the snow peas are crisp-tender and the kale turns bright green and starts to wilt and soften, about 2 minutes.

"It can take a few tries to get the hang of it, but believe me, you'll know it's worth it when you bite into your first mouthful of stir-fry goodness. I love adding fresh foraged greens and mushrooms from around my cabin; it doesn't get more local than that!" –LEAH

Cheese Cauliflower

FROM THE KITCHEN OF: **PAM**

YIELD: **MAKES 4 TO 6 SERVINGS**

My pa didn't cook often, but when he did, it sure was tasty! This here was my favorite dish of his; it's simple but delicious, and it brings back a lot of good memories every time I make it. And there's so many different kinds of cheese out there these days that I think I've actually made the recipe better!

The trick is to blend some of the cauliflower right into the cheese sauce to give it a smooth, creamy texture. We didn't have a fancy blender or anything like that when I was a girl, so Pa just used a potato masher and worked it until the sauce was smooth enough. I like how smooth the blender gets it, though, and it's so much faster and easier. I dare you to just eat one bite. Betcha can't!

INGREDIENTS

3 tablespoons **UNSALTED BUTTER**

½ cup **PANKO**

KOSHER SALT and **FRESHLY GROUND BLACK PEPPER**

2 large **CAULIFLOWERS** (4½ to 5 lb total), leaves and core removed, then cut into large florets

1⅓ cups **WHOLE MILK**

1½ tablespoons **ALL-PURPOSE FLOUR**

2 **GARLIC CLOVES**, minced

¼ teaspoon chopped **FRESH THYME LEAVES**

3 ounces **HAVARTI CHEESE**, shredded (about 1 cup)

3 ounces **GRUYÈRE CHEESE**, shredded (about 1 cup)

3 tablespoons **EXTRA-VIRGIN OLIVE OIL**

2 tablespoons grated **PARMESAN CHEESE**

Place 2 racks in the upper and bottom positions in the oven, and place a baking sheet on each. Preheat the oven to 450°F.

In a large saucepan over medium heat, melt half the butter until bubbly. Add the panko, a large pinch of salt, and several grinds of pepper. Toast the panko, stirring frequently, until golden brown and crispy, 6 to 8 minutes. Pour the crumbs into a small bowl.

Rinse out the saucepan (no need to wipe dry) and fill it halfway with water. Add 2 cups (6 oz) of the cauliflower and a large pinch of salt, bring to a boil over medium-high heat, and cook for 7 to 9 minutes. Reduce the heat to low, cover with a lid, and simmer until the cauliflower is very soft, about 15 minutes. Drain well. Add the cauliflower to a blender along with the milk and blend until very smooth.

In the same saucepan (no need to clean it), melt the remaining butter over medium heat. Add the flour and garlic and cook, whisking constantly, until the garlic is softened and the flour is lightly toasted, about 2 minutes. Pour in the blended cauliflower and the thyme,

increase the heat to medium-high, and bring to a simmer, about 5 minutes, whisking frequently. Reduce the heat to medium and cook, whisking frequently, until the sauce is thickened to the consistency of very creamy gravy, 5 to 7 additional minutes.

Turn off the heat under the saucepan and add the Havarti and Gruyère, a handful at a time, whisking well after each addition. Continue whisking until the cheese has melted and the sauce is smooth. Season with salt and black pepper and cover with a lid to keep warm.

In a large bowl, toss the remaining cauliflower with the olive oil until well coated. Season liberally with salt and pepper, and toss once more. Divide the cauliflower between the 2 now-hot baking sheets, and roast until just tender and deeply browned in spots, about 15 minutes, giving the baking sheets a good shake and rotating them top to bottom after 10 minutes.

Spread a couple large spoonfuls of the warm cheese sauce on the bottom of a large serving platter. Scatter the roasted cauliflower on the platter, then top with the remaining sauce. Stir the Parmesan cheese into the panko and sprinkle over the cauliflower. Serve immediately.

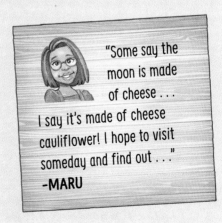

"Some say the moon is made of cheese . . . I say it's made of cheese cauliflower! I hope to visit someday and find out . . ."
-MARU

Salad

WITH WILD DANDELIONS, LEEKS, AND GRAPEFRUIT

FROM THE KITCHEN OF: **EMILY**

YIELD: **MAKES 4 TO 6 SERVINGS**

The fresh air and vibrant colors of spring always get my creative energies flowing. The other day, I took a walk into Cindersap Forest, and I could feel the dandelion greens calling to me. I think I heard them mention your name, too! The experience inspired me to make a super-healthy salad, and I wanted to share the recipe with you. While dandelions may seem like an unusual choice for a salad, they impart a wild and unique flavor that really broadens the mind. Let me know what you think!

INGREDIENTS

1 small **LEEK**

¼ cup plus 3 tablespoons **EXTRA-VIRGIN OLIVE OIL**

2 **GARLIC CLOVES**, minced

1 large branch **FRESH THYME**

KOSHER SALT and **FRESHLY GROUND BLACK PEPPER**

1 **RUBY RED GRAPEFRUIT**

2 tablespoons **WHITE WINE VINEGAR**

1 tablespoon **WHOLE-GRAIN MUSTARD**

1 teaspoon **HONEY**

1 bunch (about 5 oz), **DANDELION GREENS, LAMB'S QUARTERS, WILD ARUGULA, or OTHER FORAGED GREENS,** hand-torn into large bite-size pieces (about 8 lightly packed cups)

1 head **ENDIVE, LEAVES** separated (any large leaves cut in half)

2 small **CARROTS**, thinly sliced diagonally

½ cup **FRESH FLAT-LEAF PARSLEY**

44

"There's no quicker way to my heart than with gifts of fresh, green salad . . . though I could probably eat only two a week!" –LEAH

Trim the tough green top from the leek (reserve or freeze to make Vegetable Stock, page 25, if desired), slice the leek in half lengthwise, then cut the halves in half again. Cut the leeks into ⅛-inch slices. Transfer the leek to a medium bowl, fill the bowl with cold water, and use your hands to separate the pieces and coax out any dirt. Drain through a fine-mesh strainer until there is no dirt left remaining. Spread the leek on a towel to dry.

In a medium skillet over medium-low heat, warm ¼ cup of the olive oil, then add the leek and the garlic and thyme. Season with salt and pepper, and cook, stirring occasionally, until the leek is very tender but not browned, 15 to 20 minutes. Remove the thyme, then transfer the mixture to a medium bowl and let cool completely.

Meanwhile, slice the top and bottom off of the grapefruit so it can sit flat on a cutting board. Slice along the curve of the fruit from top to bottom to remove the peel and pith. Working over a medium bowl to catch any juices, use a small paring knife to cut between the membranes to release the grapefruit

segments. Place the segments in a small bowl. Squeeze any remaining juice from the fruit into the medium bowl.

Into the bowl with the leek and olive oil, pour ¼ cup of the grapefruit juice (drink the rest or save for another use). Add the vinegar, mustard, honey, and a pinch of salt and pepper. Slowly whisk in the remaining 3 tablespoons olive oil to make a vinaigrette.

In a large bowl, combine the dandelion greens, endive, carrots, and parsley. Drizzle with half the vinaigrette, season to taste with salt and pepper, and toss gently to combine. Transfer half the salad to a large serving platter and nestle half the grapefruit segments in the greens. Scatter the remaining salad on top, add the remaining grapefruit sections, and drizzle with additional vinaigrette. Serve immediately.

Queen's Tip
When you've finished all your gathering, treat yourself to a delightful Spring Foragers' Feast by combining Chowder, page 26, this salad, and Fiddlehead Risotto, page 28!

Rice Pudding

WITH CHERRY COMPOTE

FROM THE KITCHEN OF: **EVELYN**

YIELD: **MAKES 4 TO 6 SERVINGS**

Some folks say rice is bland or boring, but I say those folks don't have any imagination. There are so many tasty things you can make with rice, and all it takes is a little milk and sugar to turn those fluffy little grains into a delicious dessert! Cooking the mixture down slowly gives the rice a soft, chewy texture that suits its sweetness perfectly. It'll put a smile on even the biggest grump's face, and I should know!

You'll probably want to dig in right away, but it's important to let the pudding cool and set completely; chill it in the fridge for the best flavor. It's delicious on its own, but when topped with a sweet cherry compote, this rice pudding recipe is just heavenly!

INGREDIENTS

⅔ cup **LONG-GRAIN WHITE RICE**

4 cups **WHOLE MILK**, plus more as needed

½ **VANILLA BEAN**

2 tablespoons **UNSALTED BUTTER**

1 cup **WATER**

½ cup **GRANULATED SUGAR**

KOSHER SALT

CHERRY COMPOTE (recipe follows)

TOASTED SLICED ALMONDS, for serving

RECIPE CONTINUES RECIPE CONTINUES

Put the rice into a fine-mesh strainer and quickly rinse with cold water. (You are just trying to wash away any dirt or debris left on the rice, not rinse away the starch.) Set the rice aside to dry slightly, about 15 minutes.

Place the 4 cups of milk in a medium bowl. Slice the half-pod of vanilla in half lengthwise and use the back of a paring knife or butter knife to scrape out the seeds. Place the seeds and the scraped pod into the milk. Give it a good stir to combine, then set aside.

In a medium saucepan over medium heat, melt the butter. Add the rice and cook, stirring frequently, until the rice is opaque and bright white and the butter has become very foamy, 5 to 7 minutes. Add the vanilla milk (including the pod), the water, sugar, and a good pinch of salt. Bring the mixture to a simmer, stirring and scraping the saucepan occasionally, 20 to 25 minutes. (Do not rush this process; you do not want to scorch the milk.) Continue to cook, adjusting the heat as needed to maintain a simmer, until the rice is very plump and tender and the milk has thickened and coats the grains of rice, 25 to 35 additional minutes, stirring frequently.

Remove the saucepan from the heat and scoop the rice pudding into a medium bowl. Let cool at room temperature for 1 hour, stirring occasionally. (The pudding will thicken significantly as it cools.) Cover the bowl and transfer to the refrigerator to chill for at least 1 hour and up to 5 days. Once chilled, the rice pudding will be thick; if you prefer a thinner consistency, stir in additional milk (a splash at a time) until the pudding is perfect for you.

Remove the vanilla bean from the pudding and scoop the pudding into 4 to 6 small serving bowls. Top with spoonfuls of the cherry compote, then sprinkle with the toasted sliced almonds. Serve.

CHERRY COMPOTE

Makes about 1½ cups

1 pound sweet red cherries (about 3½ cups), stems removed and fruit pitted and halved

¼ cup fresh mandarin juice (from about 2 small mandarins)

3 to 4 tablespoons granulated sugar

Kosher salt

In a medium saucepan over medium heat, combine the cherries, mandarin juice, sugar (amount depends on your preference and how sweet the cherries are), and a pinch of salt. Stir to combine, and bring the mixture to a simmer, stirring occasionally and adjusting the heat as needed to maintain the simmer, until the cherries are softened but still hold their shape, 15 to 20 minutes more. Spoon a little more than half the cherries into a medium bowl. Continue to simmer the remaining cherries and fruit juices until the mixture reduces by about half and becomes a syrupy, glossy sauce, about 10 additional minutes.

Pour the sauce over the cherries in the bowl, stir to combine, and let cool completely. The compote will thicken as it cools. Use the cooled compote right away or transfer it to an airtight container and store in the refrigerator for up to 7 days.

"I have performed a spectrographic analysis of this sample and have determined it to be an optimal energy source for my body. However, I may need 200 additional grams for . . . further analysis in my private laboratory." -DEMETRIUS

Rhubarb Pie

FROM THE KITCHEN OF: **MARNIE**

YIELD: **MAKES 8 TO 10 SERVINGS**

It's always been my opinion that a rhubarb pie should taste like rhubarb, with just enough sugar to balance out its tartness. There's a place for strawberries or vanilla, but that place is not in my rhubarb pie. A buttery, flaky crust filled to the brim with fresh rhubarb . . . nothing says spring quite like it! The sugar and flour mix with the rhubarb as the pie bakes, creating a sweet and tangy filling that has to be tasted to be believed. And remember to use butter only from happy cows; happy cows make happy milk, which makes happy butter. It's a fact!

INGREDIENTS

2⅔ cups (370 g) and 7 tablespoons (60 g) **ALL-PURPOSE FLOUR**, plus more for dusting

1 cup plus 2 tablespoons (200 g) **GRANULATED SUGAR**

KOSHER SALT

1 cup (2 sticks; 220 g) frozen **UNSALTED BUTTER**

½ cup (120 ml) **ICE WATER**

1 tablespoon **FRESH LEMON JUICE**

1½ pounds (680 g) **FRESH RHUBARB STALKS**, cut crosswise into ¼-inch (6 mm) pieces

2 tablespoons room-temperature **BUTTER**, for filling

1 **LARGE EGG**

1 tablespoon **RAW** or **TURBINADO SUGAR**, for sprinkling (optional)

RECIPE CONTINUES

49

In a large bowl, stir together 2⅔ cups (370 g) of the flour, 2 tablespoons of the sugar, and ¾ teaspoon salt. Whisk to combine.

Grate the frozen butter on the large holes of a box grater, then add to the flour mixture and use your fingers to work the butter into the flour until it resembles coarse crumbs.

Stir together the ice water and lemon juice, and drizzle 5 tablespoons (75 ml) of it over the flour mixture. Use your hands to mix until you have a rough dough that holds together when you squeeze it in your hand; add more water, 1 teaspoon at a time, if needed.

Lay out 2 large pieces of plastic wrap and divide the dough evenly between them. Press each portion into a mostly smooth dough and flatten into a disk 1 inch (2.5 cm) thick. Wrap both disks tightly, then chill in the refrigerator until firm (but not hard), about 1 hour.

In a large bowl, toss together the rhubarb, ⅔ cup (130 g) of the sugar, and ¼ teaspoon salt. Let macerate while the dough chills, about 1 hour, stirring occasionally. The sugar will melt and create a syrup that coats the rhubarb.

On a lightly floured surface, roll out 1 dough disk into a 12-inch (30 cm) round, about ⅛ inch (3 mm) thick. Carefully roll the dough around the rolling pin, then unroll into a 9-inch (23 cm) pie plate. Press the crust into the pie plate, then trim the overhang, leaving ½ inch (1.3 cm) around the edges. Place in the refrigerator to chill while you finish the filling and roll out the second dough disk.

Sprinkle the remaining 7 tablespoons (60 g) flour over the rhubarb and stir until well combined and there are no clumps of flour. Set aside to thicken slightly.

Roll out the remaining dough disk into a 12-inch (30 cm) round about ⅛ inch (3 mm) thick. Use a 1½-inch (4 cm) star-shaped cookie cutter to cut out a star in the center of the dough (alternatively, you can use a small paring knife to cut out the star shape).

Stir the remaining ⅓ cup (65 g) of sugar into the rhubarb filling, then spoon into the chilled bottom crust. Cut the butter for the filling into small cubes and press evenly into the rhubarb. Carefully roll the top crust around the rolling pin, then unroll and drape over the rhubarb. Trim the top crust so that it is just slightly larger than the bottom crust. Fold the edge over and crimp around the edge as desired. Chill the pie in the refrigerator for 30 minutes.

Place a baking sheet on the bottom rack of the oven and preheat the oven to 425°F (220°C).

In a small bowl, whisk together the egg and a splash of water. Brush onto the pie crust, then sprinkle with the turbinado sugar, if desired. Place the pie on the baking sheet and bake for 15 minutes. Rotate the baking sheet and reduce the oven temperature to 375°F (190°C). Continue to bake until the crust is golden brown and the filling is vigorously bubbling (you should be able to see it bubbling through the star opening in the center of the pie), about 1 additional hour, rotating the baking sheet once more after 30 minutes. Remove from the oven and cool completely on the hot baking sheet, 4 to 5 hours.

When the pie has cooled, slice into 8 to 10 wedges and serve.

"I'm happy to share cakes and cookies with Kent and the kids, but I won't let them get their hands on my rhubarb pie!" -JODI

Ginger Ale

FROM THE KITCHEN OF: **VOLCANO DWARF**

YIELD: **MAKES 4 TO 6 SERVINGS**

Translated from the Dwarvish:

You humans have been using the rhizome of the ginger plant for myriad purposes since ancient times. But we dwarves have been using it for far, far longer. Yes, it helps to soothe a discomforted stomach, but its true powers are multifarious and resplendent. Perhaps someday, when you have shown yourselves to be worthy, we will share our knowledge. For now, though, take comfort in the fact that ginger relieves an upset stomach, and allow me to teach you how to prepare a piquant sparkling beverage from it known as ginger ale.

There are different ways to prepare this concoction, but I'll stick with one of the easier ones for now. This method extracts a concentrated syrup from the ginger, which can then be combined with bubbling water just before serving. It's a very old dwarvish technique, but there's no reason to be intimidated; simply follow the steps and you'll be successful.

INGREDIENTS

1 (6-inch) piece of **FRESH GINGER**, peeled

4 long strips of **LIME ZEST**

⅔ cup **WATER**

⅓ cup **GRANULATED SUGAR**

⅓ cup **HONEY**

ICE CUBES, as needed

3 cups **PLAIN SELTZER**

4 **LIME WEDGES**

Thinly slice half the ginger and place in a small saucepan along with the lime zest, water, sugar, and honey. Stir to combine, then place over low heat and slowly bring to a low simmer, stirring occasionally, 15 to 25 minutes. Remove the saucepan from the heat and let the syrup cool completely.

Finely grate the remaining ginger into a small bowl (this helps catch all the juice). Scrape the grated ginger and juices (about 3 tablespoons) into the cool syrup and give it a good stir. Strain through a sieve into a small bowl, pressing down on the pulp to extract as much liquid as possible.

Divide the syrup among 4 tall glasses. Transfer the remaining syrup to a glass jar with a lid, where it can be stored in the refrigerator for up to 14 days. Fill the glasses with ice cubes, then top with the seltzer. Use a long spoon to give each glass a good stir, then top each with a lime wedge. Serve immediately.

"Now this is worth waking up for. Bring me another glass and maybe we'll see about getting you an early reward or two." -GIL

"The bubbles make me sneeze, but it's kinda fun! Sometimes Mom makes me drink some ginger ale when I don't feel good, and it helps. Don't tell Mom, but sometimes I pretend to have a tummyache just so she'll give me a glass of ginger ale. It's yummy!"
-VINCENT

SUMMER

A festival of flavors

If nature played a song, then summer would be its crescendo. It's a time of growth, abundance, sunlight, and most important, a wide variety of culinary opportunities. Fresh fish, juicy fruits, rich summer milk, and much more are just waiting to be enjoyed.

As temperatures begin to soar, you'll no doubt be looking for refreshing options for appetizers, entrées, or something to bring to your local Luau Festival! Well, dare I say, you've come to the right place. Need a finger food to whet your guests' appetites? Make some loaves of fresh-baked Bread, then slice them, toast the slices, and serve up a platter of refreshing tomato and herb Bruschetta! How about a tropical-themed spread? I've got you covered! Everyone will be talking all summer long about your feast of Tropical Curry, served up alongside an ice-cold Piña Colada, and Mango Sticky Rice for dessert.

Summer is also a time of bounty for all my seafood lovers out there. Warmer waters mean bigger fishing hauls, and so the variety and quality of fish are at their peak. Impress your guests with Fish Tacos on every plate, or maybe get everyone involved in making their own Maki Rolls with their favorite fish and other fillings. Hosting a party with a fancier theme? Crab Cakes and Shrimp Cocktail will make everyone at the table feel like royalty! Whether the dish is raw or cooked, baked or grilled, we've got something for every one of you.

Tropical delicacies and seafood delights abound under the summer sun. So, what are you waiting for? The great outdoors are calling!

Bread and Bruschetta

FROM THE KITCHEN OF: **THE QUEEN OF SAUCE** YIELD: **MAKES 4 SERVINGS**

Nothing says summer quite like a fresh, juicy tomato. And what better way to showcase its bold personality than to set it atop a simple crust of bread? Here, I'll show you how to do just that! First, we'll whip up a batch of crusty baguettes. Then we'll slice and toast them, and top them with sun-ripened tomatoes, garlic, basil, and a drizzle of extra-virgin olive oil. Ahh . . . now that's the taste of summer!

For novice chefs, breadmaking can be an intimidating prospect, but it's really much easier than it might first seem. There aren't many ingredients to worry about, and when the time comes for the dough to rise, the yeast does all the work for you. With a little practice, you'll be impressing all your friends with your masterful breadmaking skills!

BREAD

Makes 4 small baguettes

1⅓ cups (315 ml) lukewarm water

2 teaspoons honey

1½ teaspoons active dry yeast

**2½ cups (350 g) all-purpose flour,
plus more for dusting**

¾ cup (105 g) whole wheat flour

Kosher salt

1⅔ cups (395 ml) water

Extra-virgin olive oil, for greasing

In a large bowl, whisk together the lukewarm water and honey until smooth. Whisk in the yeast and let the mixture sit until foamy, about 10 minutes.

To the bowl add the all-purpose flour, whole wheat flour, and 2½ teaspoons salt and stir with a wooden spoon or rubber spatula until the mixture comes together to form a shaggy dough. Using your hands, mix until the dough forms a somewhat rough ball; the dough will seem dry at this point, and that is okay. Cover the dough and let it sit at room temperature for 15 minutes. (This short resting time will allow the dough to absorb some of the liquid and makes it easier to knead.)

Lightly grease a large bowl with olive oil. Turn out the dough onto a lightly floured work surface and knead until the dough is smooth and elastic, 8 to 10 minutes. Transfer the dough ball to the greased bowl, turn to coat in the oil, cover the bowl, and set aside at room temperature until doubled in size, about 1 hour.

Use your hands to gently deflate the dough ball and fold its rounded edges into the center of the dough. Turn the folded dough over, cover the bowl again, and let it sit until it nearly doubles in size again, about 45 minutes.

Gently deflate the dough ball again and fold its rounded edges into the center of the dough. Turn the folded dough over, cover the bowl, and let it sit until it nearly doubles in size once more, about 45 additional minutes.

Place a piece of parchment paper on a large baking sheet (if your baking sheet is rimless, then no need to invert) and lightly flour the paper. Transfer the dough to a lightly floured work surface, shape into a roughly 6-inch (15 cm) square, and cut into 4 equal pieces. Working with one piece of dough at a time, use your fingers to press the dough into a rough rectangle about ½ inch (1.3 cm) thick, with the longer side closest to you. Fold the top and bottom of the dough toward the middle so that the edges just slightly overlap, then use your fingers to seal the seam. Repeat this flattening and folding technique once more. The dough should have folded to a log roughly 10 inches (25 cm) long. The ends of the log should be pretty rounded, but if not, use your hand to push them into a more rounded shape. Place the log seam side down on the baking sheet.

Repeat the shaping process with the 3 remaining pieces of dough, spacing the logs evenly apart on the baking sheet. Use your fingers to gently lift up the parchment paper between the logs so it helps hold the log shape (the paper should look like waves between the logs). Use 2 long, heavy objects (rolling pins or wine bottles work well) to hold up the

"Ah, tomato . . . like a gentle breeze atop a jagged mountain of crunchy bread. There's something poetic about the juxtaposition, no?" –ELLIOTT

parchment on the outside of the outer loaves, then place 2 heavy cans to hold the rolling pins in place. This mimics a baking couche, which is what professional bakers use to help retain the long, narrow shape of the baguettes as they rise. (If you happen to have a couche, feel free to use it here.) Let the loaves sit, uncovered, until they become very puffy, with the squishiness of a jumbo marshmallow, about 1 hour. The dough will rise and appear more loaf-like, but it will not necessarily double in size.

About 40 minutes into the final resting, place a medium cast-iron skillet on the lowest rack of the oven, then place a second rack in the center of the oven. Put an inverted large rimmed baking sheet on the center rack and preheat the oven to 450°F (230°C).

Pour the 1⅔ cups (395 ml) of water into a small saucepan and start to bring to a boil over medium heat.

Remove the cans and rolling pins from the baking sheet, then flatten the parchment paper. Use a sharp knife (or a baker's lame—a special curved blade—if you have it) to make 4 diagonal slices, each ½ inch (1.3 cm) deep, along the top of each loaf.

Using the inverted baking sheet as a makeshift pizza peel, open the oven and put the baking sheet with the bread loaves alongside the inverted baking sheet. Carefully pull out the parchment paper below the loaves, shuttling the loaves onto the hot baking sheet. Working quickly, pour the boiling water into the skillet on the bottom rack, and quickly shut the oven door. The steam created by the water will help the baguettes rise nicely in the oven.

Bake the baguettes until they are a deep golden brown and crusty, about 20 minutes. Meanwhile, set a wire rack into a large rimmed baking sheet.

Remove the inverted baking sheet with the loaves on it and the cast-iron skillet. Transfer the baguettes to the rack and return the baguettes to the oven, with heat turned off. Crack the oven door open by a couple of inches and let the baguettes cool completely in the oven, 1½ to 2 hours (the timing will depend on how quickly your oven reaches room temperature).

The baguettes are ready to be served. Two loaves are used for the Bruschetta.

BRUSCHETTA

Makes 4 to 8 servings

**1 pound (450 g) ripe tomatoes
(mix of varietal and color works well)**

Kosher salt

5 tablespoons (75 ml) extra-virgin olive oil

1½ tablespoons red wine vinegar

2 Bread baguettes (preceding recipe)

2 large garlic cloves

**¼ cup (4 g) lightly packed hand-torn
fresh basil leaves**

Flaky sea salt

Preheat the oven to 375°F (190°C).

Core and chop the tomatoes into roughly ½-inch (1.3 cm) pieces. Place in a medium bowl, sprinkle with 1 teaspoon salt, then stir gently. Set the tomatoes aside until they become very juicy, about 15 minutes, stirring occasionally.

Spoon out 3 tablespoons of the tomato water and set aside.

Stir 2 tablespoons of the olive oil and the vinegar into the tomatoes.

Cut the baguettes diagonally into ½-inch (1.3 cm) slices, making 24 to 28 slices. Spread the slices on a large baking sheet in a single layer. Brush both sides of the slices with the remaining 3 tablespoons olive oil and season

with salt. Bake until crispy on both sides and browned around some of the edges, about 20 minutes, flipping once after 10 minutes. Let the slices cool on the baking sheet until you can handle them, at least 5 minutes.

Cut the garlic cloves in half crosswise, then rub the top sides of the toasted bread with the cut sides of the garlic. Brush the slices with the reserved salted tomato water. Stir the basil into the tomato mixture. Taste for seasoning and adjust with more salt, if needed.

With a slotted spoon, scoop the tomato mixture onto the slices (or use a regular spoon and tilt it against the side of the bowl to help drain away the juices), dividing the mixture evenly. Top with a light drizzle of the tomato juices remaining on the bottom of the bowl; then sprinkle with flaky sea salt and serve immediately.

Bread and Bruschetta
58

Maki
Roll
64

Maki Roll

FROM THE KITCHEN OF: **THE QUEEN OF SAUCE**

YIELD: **MAKES 6 ROLLS** (48 pieces total)

Ah, the maki roll. It's a treasure trove of flavors, the delightful light sweetness of the sushi rice frolicking with your favorite ingredients in that chewy nori wrapper, sliced into perfect little mouthfuls. Sure, there are plenty of tried-and-true traditional maki rolls out there, but there are no rules when it comes to what you put in your own rolls. As long as you've got that delectable vinegared rice and nori to wrap it all up, you've got a maki roll. Use your imagination!

Be sure to use only the freshest sushi-grade fish if you'll be eating it raw; there are also countless options for cooked fish—or no fish at all! Here, we'll be making a spicy salmon filling that's sure to please, along with cucumber and avocado to balance out the heat. Dip each piece in soy sauce with a bit of wasabi, and you're in for a treat!

INGREDIENTS

1½ cups good-quality **JAPANESE SHORT-GRAIN RICE**

1½ cups **WATER**

½ cup finely diced **CARROT**

¼ cup **UNSEASONED RICE WINE VINEGAR**

1 tablespoon **GRANULATED SUGAR**

KOSHER SALT

12 ounces skinless **SUSHI-GRADE SALMON FILLET**

3 tablespoons **MAYONNAISE**

2 to 3 teaspoons **ASIAN CHILI SAUCE**, such as sriracha, as desired

½ teaspoon toasted **SESAME OIL**

2 thinly sliced **SCALLIONS** (white and green parts)

6 full-size **ROASTED NORI SHEETS**

1 large **PERSIAN CUCUMBER**, thinly sliced into matchsticks

1 ripe **AVOCADO**, halved, seed removed, sliced lengthwise into 18 pieces

PICKLED GINGER, WASABI, and **SOY SAUCE**, for serving

Put the rice into a large fine-mesh strainer and rinse under cold running water until the water runs clear. Place the rice and the 1½ cups water in a medium saucepan and soak the rice for 30 minutes.

After 30 minutes, place the saucepan on medium-high heat and bring to a boil, then reduce the heat to low, cover the saucepan with a tight-fitting lid, and simmer until all the water has been absorbed by the rice, about 20 minutes. Turn off the heat, quickly lift the lid, and sprinkle the top of the rice with the carrots. Return the lid and let the rice steam in the residual heat for 10 minutes.

Meanwhile, in a small bowl, combine the vinegar, sugar, and 1 teaspoon salt. Stir until the sugar and salt are dissolved.

Wet a rice paddle or rubber spatula and gently mix the rice and carrots in the saucepan. Transfer the mixture to a large bowl, drizzle half the sushi vinegar over the rice, and use the rice paddle or rubber spatula to fold the vinegar into the rice. Drizzle with the remaining sushi vinegar and continue to gently stir until the rice completely absorbs the vinegar, about 2 minutes. Cover the rice with a damp kitchen towel and set aside to cool completely, about 30 minutes.

Finely dice the salmon and place in a medium bowl. Add the mayonnaise, chili sauce, sesame oil, a large pinch of salt, and the scallions. Gently stir to combine, then cover and refrigerate the salmon.

When ready to serve, place a sushi mat or piece of parchment paper cut into a 12-inch square on a clean work surface. Arrange 1 sheet of nori, rough side up, on the mat with the longer side nearest to you. Using damp hands, gently press one-sixth (about ⅔ cup) of the sushi rice onto the nori in a single, even layer, leaving a 1-inch border on the side farthest from you and

a ½-inch border on the side nearest to you. The rice should reach the edges of the nori on both the left and the right sides.

Make a thin line of sliced cucumber just below the center of the rice, then place 3 pieces of avocado on the rice directly above the cucumber. Spoon one-sixth (about a scant ⅓ cup) of the spicy salmon on top of the cucumber and avocado, using your fingers to lightly press the salmon together so it is slightly compressed. (This will make the rolling process much easier.)

Starting with the side nearest to you, use the ½ inch of exposed seaweed to lift the rice tightly over the filling. Use your fingers to tuck the edge of the seaweed underneath the filling, then use the sushi mat to continue to tightly roll the maki roll. When you reach the end of the nori, use your hands to tighten the mat around the roll. (This will help to shape and seal the roll to ensure the filling stays intact.)

Slice the maki roll crosswise into 8 equal pieces and transfer to a large serving platter or an individual plate. Repeat with the remaining ingredients to make a total of 6 maki rolls.

Serve immediately with some pickled ginger, wasabi, and soy sauce on the side.

"You humans have the strangest eating habits. You put fish and vegetables on rice, and wrap it in seaweed? Odd, but tasty!" -DWARF

Fruit Salad

FROM THE KITCHEN OF: **THE QUEEN OF SAUCE**

YIELD: **MAKES 4 TO 6 SERVINGS**

What could be more refreshing than a bowl of cool, juicy fruit on a hot summer's day? Don't worry, it's a trick question! Now, obviously, we aren't just going to toss some fruit into a bowl and call it a day. No, we'll be giving our fruit the royal treatment, with apricot wedges poached in a luscious vanilla-infused syrup. The soft, sweet apricots beautifully complement the crisp freshness of the honeydew and watermelon. Then we'll round out the flavor profile with the wonderful, subtle tartness of blueberries.

And there's no way we're letting that syrup go to waste, no sir! That sweet vanilla (and now apricot-infused) syrup is going right on that yummy fruit—just don't forget to remove the pits beforehand! This is a next-level dessert that works just as well as an afternoon snack. It'll pick you up and cool you down!

INGREDIENTS

½ **VANILLA BEAN**

1 cup (8 fl oz) **DRY WHITE WINE**

1 cup **WATER**

½ cup **GRANULATED SUGAR**

4 medium-ripe **APRICOTS** (about 12 oz), pitted and quartered, with pits reserved (see Queen's Tip)

4 cups ripe **HONEYDEW BALLS**

6 cups (1-inch) **WATERMELON** cubes

8 ounces **BLUEBERRIES** (about 1½ cups)

FRESH MINT LEAVES, for garnish

Queen's Tip

Instead of apricots, you can use 3 small nectarines or peaches and cut them into 6 wedges each.

Slice the vanilla pod in half lengthwise and use the back of a paring knife or butter knife to scrape out the seeds. Place the seeds and the scraped pod in a medium saucepan. Add the wine, water, sugar, and apricot pits. Place over medium heat and bring to a simmer, stirring occasionally, 5 to 8 minutes. Add the apricots and continue to simmer, stirring occasionally, until the apricots are just tender, 4 to 7 minutes, depending on the size and ripeness of the fruit.

Use a slotted spoon to transfer the apricots to a small bowl or dish. Increase the heat to medium-high and bring the poaching liquid to a boil. Cook, stirring occasionally, until reduced by half (to about 1 cup), about 10 minutes. Remove the pits (but leave the vanilla pod), then pour the syrup over the apricots. Let cool slightly at room temperature, then transfer to the refrigerator and chill completely.

In a large bowl, combine the honeydew, watermelon, and blueberries. Remove the vanilla pod from the syrup, then use a spoon to drizzle ½ cup of the syrup over the melons and blueberries. Stir gently to combine, then transfer to a large serving bowl or platter and nestle the poached apricots into the dressed fruit. Drizzle with more of the syrup, garnish with the mint, and serve.

"This is even better than the fancy fruit salads they serve at those overpriced shops in Zuzu City. If I'd known it was so easy to make my own at home, I wouldn't have wasted my money!" -HALEY

Tropical Curry

FROM THE KITCHEN OF: GUS

YIELD: MAKES 4 TO 6 SERVINGS

Here, I've got a fun idea for your next luau or summer gathering: a spicy, fragrant curry full of potatoes and pineapple. Sound good? Well, let's make it even better by serving it in bowls made out of pineapples. I figured that'd get your attention! We'll add some heat with a single Scotch Bonnet chile and a bit of hot sauce, then serve up the curry with additional hot sauce on the side. That way, everyone can add more if they really want to channel their inner lava eel!

You'll need only 1 cup of pineapple for the curry itself; the rest of the pineapples are hollowed out and made into the serving bowls. If you don't want to go to the trouble, you can just use regular bowls (in that case, you will need only 1 cup of pineapple for the curry). But all that delicious pineapple would make an excellent dessert or a strong base for a fruit salad. Think about it!

INGREDIENTS

2 to 3 large ripe **PINEAPPLES**

2 tablespoons **UNREFINED COCONUT OIL**

1 large **YELLOW ONION**, coarsely chopped

KOSHER SALT

1 large **RED BELL PEPPER**, coarsely chopped

1 **SCOTCH BONNET CHILE** (or **SERRANO** or **JALAPEÑO**) **PEPPER**, seeded (if desired), and finely chopped

5 **GARLIC CLOVES**, minced

1 (1-inch) piece **FRESH GINGER**, peeled and finely minced

2 teaspoons chopped **FRESH THYME LEAVES**

¼ cup **JAMAICAN CURRY POWDER**

2 cups **VEGETABLE STOCK** (page 25)

1 (13.5 oz) can **UNSWEETENED COCONUT MILK**

2 to 4 dashes **JAMAICAN HOT SAUCE**, plus more for serving

1 pound **YUKON GOLD POTATOES**, unpeeled, cut into ¾-inch chunks

12 ounces **SWEET POTATOES**, peeled and cut into ¾-inch chunks

Steamed **LONG-GRAIN WHITE RICE**, hot

Coarsely chopped **FRESH CILANTRO LEAVES** and **SOFT STEMS**, for garnish

"I'm not usually a big fan of spicy foods, but I can't get enough of this curry! Maybe it's the sweetness of the pineapple and coconut milk, but give me a bowl of this with a glass of Gus's iced mango green tea, and I'm instantly transported to the relaxing shores of Ginger Island." —CAROLINE

On a large cutting board, lay 1 pineapple on its side. Cut off and discard the green top, being careful to slice right under the base of the leaves. Cut the pineapple in half crosswise. Stand each pineapple half cut side up to ensure that it stands up straight, without wobbling. If they tend to wobble, trim the bottoms as little as needed until they sit straight (minimal trimming, only).

Use a small paring knife to cut around the edges of the pineapple flesh, leaving a ½-inch border of flesh all around. Cut the center of the pineapple into fourths, then use a spoon to scoop out the flesh, leaving a thick layer at the bottom of the pineapple, about 1 inch. Cut away the pieces of core and finely chop enough of the pineapple to measure 1 cup. At this point, the pineapple flesh should resemble canned crushed pineapple.

Place the chopped pineapple in a fine-mesh strainer set over a bowl to drain the pineapple juice and set aside. (Reserve any extra pineapple flesh and juice for another use.) Place the 2 pineapple "bowls" on a large baking sheet or platter. Repeat this process to make 2 to 4 additional pineapple "bowls."

In a small Dutch oven set on medium to medium-high heat, warm the coconut oil. When the oil is hot, add the onion, season with salt, and cook, stirring occasionally, until softened, about 10 minutes. Add the bell pepper and chile pepper, season with salt, and cook, stirring occasionally, until crisp-tender, 6 to 8 minutes. Add the garlic, ginger, and thyme and cook, stirring constantly, until softened, 2 to 3 minutes. Add the curry powder and ¼ cup of stock, stir to combine, and cook, stirring constantly, for 2 minutes.

Add the remaining stock, the coconut milk, and hot sauce, and stir until smooth. Add the Yukon Gold and the sweet potatoes, and bring to a simmer, stirring occasionally, about 10 minutes. Lower the heat to medium and continue to cook at a gentle simmer (adjusting the heat as needed) until the potatoes are fork-tender (but not falling apart), 30 to 40 additional minutes, stirring occasionally. Stir in the chopped pineapple and cook, stirring occasionally, until the pineapple is heated through, about 2 minutes. Season with additional salt, if needed.

Place a small scoop of hot rice in the bottom of each pineapple bowl and top with some of the curry. Sprinkle with the cilantro (if using) and serve immediately, with additional hot sauce on the side.

Queen's Tip

If you would like to add seafood to the curry, nestle bite-size pieces of skinless firm whitefish or peeled and deveined whole shrimp in the curry before you add the pineapple, and then simmer until the fish or shrimp is just cooked through, about 3 minutes. You might have to add a splash of additional stock to ensure that the seafood has enough liquid to cook in.

Tropical
Curry
68

Lucky Lunch

SHRIMP CEVICHE ON A BED OF GREENS

FROM THE KITCHEN OF: **THE QUEEN OF SAUCE**

YIELD: **MAKES 4 SERVINGS**

If you've been on the hunt for the perfect seafood lunch, then you're in luck! A tangy mix of poached shrimp and fresh vegetables nestled between two star-shaped toasted tortillas delivers a cool, refreshing blast of seafood flavor with every bite. The tortilla stars can be broken up into chips as you eat, or if you're feeling especially adventurous—and have plenty of napkins handy—you can try eating the whole thing like a sandwich. After you've cleaned your plate, you're bound to feel like the spirits are smiling down on you all day long!

INGREDIENTS

6 cups (1½ quarts) **WATER**

½ cup **FRESH LIME JUICE** (from about 4 juicy limes)

KOSHER SALT

12 ounces large or extra-large **SHRIMP**, peeled, deveined, and tails removed

5 tablespoons **EXTRA-VIRGIN OLIVE OIL**

¾ teaspoon **GRANULATED SUGAR**

2 **GARLIC CLOVES**, grated

½ small **RED ONION**, finely chopped

1 small **JALAPEÑO**, halved, seeded (if desired), and thinly sliced

1 large **PERSIAN CUCUMBER**, quartered lengthwise and cut into ½-inch pieces

1 cup **RAINBOW CHERRY TOMATOES**, quartered

12 (6½-inch) **YELLOW CORN TORTILLAS**

1 small **AVOCADO**, halved, pit removed, cut into ½-inch cubes

3 tablespoons thinly sliced **FRESH CHIVE GREENS**, plus flowers for garnish (see Queen's Tips)

¼ cup coarsely chopped **FRESH CILANTRO LEAVES** and **SOFT STEMS**

2 packed cups thinly sliced **ROMAINE LETTUCE**

Special Equipment
6-inch **STAR STENCIL** (see Queen's Tips)

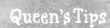

In a large saucepan over medium-high heat, bring the water to a boil. Stir in 2 tablespoons of the lime juice and 1 tablespoon of salt, then add the shrimp. Cover with a lid and immediately turn off the heat. Keep the shrimp in the hot liquid until just cooked through, 3 to 4 minutes. Drain and let cool slightly.

Cut the shrimp into ½-inch pieces and place in a large bowl. Add the remaining 6 tablespoons lime juice, 2 tablespoons of the olive oil, the sugar, garlic, red onion, jalapeño, cucumber, cherry tomatoes, and 1 teaspoon salt. Stir to combine, then cover and refrigerate for at least 2 hours and up to 4 hours.

Set 2 racks in the upper and lower thirds of the oven and preheat the oven to 350°F.

Stack the tortillas in 2 piles of 6 each and use a 6-inch star stencil or freehand to cut out stars (keep any scraps). Divide the tortilla stars between 2 large baking sheets, brush all over with some of the remaining olive oil, and season liberally with salt. Bake in the oven until lightly browned in spots and crispy, 15 to 20 minutes, flipping once and rotating the baking sheets top to bottom once after 10 minutes. Transfer the baked stars to a wire rack to cool. Leave the oven on.

Let the baking sheets cool completely, then wipe off any excess oil and salt. Divide the tortilla scraps between the baking sheets, spreading them out in a single layer. Brush the scraps with more of the olive oil and season liberally with salt. Bake until lightly browned in spots and crispy, about 15 minutes, flipping the scraps over and rotating the baking sheets top to bottom once after 8 minutes. Transfer the scraps to the wire rack to cool completely.

When you are ready to serve, stir the avocado, chive greens, and cilantro into the shrimp ceviche. Taste for seasoning and add more salt, if needed. To plate the Lucky Lunch, scatter one-fourth of the romaine on a large serving plate, then drizzle with some of the shrimp ceviche. Use a slotted spoon to scoop ⅓ cup of the ceviche onto the center of the lettuce, then top with 1 star tortilla chip. Layer with another scoop of ceviche, another star tortilla chip, more ceviche, and top with another star tortilla chip. Garnish with some of the chive blossoms.

Repeat to make 3 additional Lucky Lunches and serve immediately, with a bowl of the baked tortilla chips alongside.

"The spirits of luck respect those who practice their customs in earnest; this meal is the perfect example. Simply ingesting this delicacy invites a spirit into your body, bringing you good fortune for a time. But don't take my word for it; try it for yourself." **-WIZARD**

Shrimp Cocktail

FROM THE KITCHEN OF: THE QUEEN OF SAUCE

YIELD: MAKES 6 TO 8 SERVINGS

I've always had a soft spot in my heart for shrimp cocktail. There's something about the playful presentation, almost as though the shrimp are gathered around their favorite watering hole, enjoying that pungent, sweet, horseradish-y cocktail sauce. Then we swoop in and gobble them up!

Preparing the shrimp couldn't be easier; just give them a quick peel and devein them (but leave the tails on to give them built-in handles), then season and roast them. And I think we can one-up that store-bought cocktail sauce with richer flavor and a wonderful blend of spices. When everything is ready to serve, simply arrange the cooked shrimp in a ring around the rim of each serving bowl or glass, with the sauce in the middle. You can serve up individual portions, or make one big bowl of sauce decorated with lots of delicious shrimp for a party appetizer. If you double-dip, I won't tell!

INGREDIENTS

1 pound **GRAPE TOMATOES**, halved

4 **GARLIC CLOVES**, lightly smashed

1 small **SHALLOT**, thinly sliced

5 tablespoons **EXTRA-VIRGIN OLIVE OIL**

KOSHER SALT

1½ teaspoons **HONEY**

2 tablespoons **TOMATO PASTE**

Pinch of **GROUND CLOVES**

Pinch of **GROUND ALLSPICE**

2 pounds **EXTRA-JUMBO SHRIMP**, peeled and deveined, tails left on

FRESHLY GROUND BLACK PEPPER

2 to 3 packed tablespoons peeled and finely grated **FRESH HORSERADISH**, as desired

2 tablespoons **FRESH LEMON JUICE**, plus more as needed

1½ teaspoons **WORCESTERSHIRE SAUCE**

2 to 4 dashes of **HOT SAUCE**, as desired

Preheat the oven to 325°F.

In a large baking dish, combine the grape tomatoes, garlic, shallots, and 3 tablespoons of the olive oil. Season liberally with salt and stir to combine. Roast in the oven until the tomatoes are very soft, the skins are shriveled, and they have released most of their juices, about 80 minutes, stirring every 20 minutes.

Remove the tomatoes from the oven and stir in the honey, tomato paste, cloves, and allspice. Return the pan to the oven and cook for 15 additional minutes. Allow the roasted tomatoes to sit at room temperature to cool completely.

Increase the oven temperature to 425°F.

On a large rimmed baking sheet, toss the shrimp with the remaining 2 tablespoons olive oil and season with salt and pepper. Spread the shrimp in a single layer, then roast until opaque and cooked through, about 10 minutes. Transfer the shrimp to a platter to cool.

Queen's Tips

For a wonderful summer picnic feast, make these recipes, which are easy to bring along anywhere!

Bread & Bruschetta, page 58

Shrimp Cocktail, page 74

Crab Cakes, page 77

Fruit Salad, page 66

Blueberry Tart, page 92

Finish making the cocktail sauce by placing the roasted tomatoes in a food processor and blending until smooth. Spoon the mixture into a medium bowl and add the horseradish, lemon juice, Worcestershire sauce, and hot sauce. Stir until smooth and season to taste with additional lemon juice and salt, if needed. The cocktail sauce will be thick; if you prefer a thinner sauce, stir in a splash or so of water.

Transfer the cocktail sauce to a small serving bowl and serve alongside the roasted shrimp on the platter. Alternatively, spoon the cocktail sauce into individual bowls or glasses and arrange the roasted shrimp around the sides of the bowls.

"Roasted shrimp is all well and good, but I'm really just here for that sauce. I only use wild horseradish that I foraged myself, along with vine-ripened tomatoes and plenty of garlic. You can find those last two in the alley behind the Stardrop Saloon, if you're lucky." —LINUS

Crab Cakes

WITH PEACH SALSA

| FROM THE KITCHEN OF: | THE QUEEN OF SAUCE | YIELD: | MAKES 8 LARGE OR 16 SMALL CRAB CAKES |

Mmm, crab cakes, that classic seaside delicacy. Those hearty morsels, brimming with lumps of juicy crabmeat and aromatic veggies—that's my idea of comfort food! I like a little crunch in mine, so we'll use just the right amount of bell pepper and corn to give them the perfect texture. Appetizer or entrée, these crab cakes are sure to put some pep in your step.

But let's not get carried away just yet; we simply have to pair these scrumptious crab cakes with a sauce, and I have just the sauce for the job! It's a sweet salsa full of ripe summer peaches, with just a hint of heat. Of course, you're free to add more spice to yours, if you like. It's so easy to make this sauce that I bet you'll find yourself mixing up batches on the regular for all sorts of occasions. And I wouldn't blame you one bit!

INGREDIENTS

- 1 small ear of **YELLOW** or **WHITE CORN**, husked
- ⅓ cup **MAYONNAISE**
- 1 tablespoon **WHOLE-GRAIN MUSTARD**
- 1 teaspoon packed grated **FRESH LEMON ZEST**, plus 1 tablespoon **LEMON JUICE** (from 1 lemon)
- 1 teaspoon **GRANULATED GARLIC**
- ½ teaspoon **SWEET PAPRIKA**

- ¼ teaspoon **CELERY SEEDS**
- ¼ teaspoon **CAYENNE**
- 1 small **SPRING ONION**, with tops
- ½ small **RED BELL PEPPER**, cored and seeded
- 2 tablespoons **UNSALTED BUTTER**
- **KOSHER SALT** and **FRESHLY GROUND BLACK PEPPER**
- 1 **LARGE EGG**

- 2 tablespoons chopped **FRESH FLAT-LEAF PARSLEY LEAVES**
- ¾ cup **PANKO**, plus more as needed
- 1 pound **JUMBO LUMP CRABMEAT**, picked over for shell and cartilage
- **NEUTRAL HIGH-HEAT COOKING OIL, TALLOW,** or **LARD**, for pan-frying
- **PEACH SALSA** (recipe follows)

RECIPE CONTINUES

Cut the kernels off the ear of corn (about ¾ cup). Hold the corncob over a large bowl and use the back of a butter knife or spoon to scrape the milk from the cob (about 1 tablespoon). Discard the cob (or save to add to Vegetable Stock, page 25). To the bowl with the corn milk, add the mayonnaise, mustard, lemon zest and juice, granulated garlic, paprika, celery seeds, and cayenne. Stir well, then refrigerate until ready to use.

Separate the small bulb and the green tops of the spring onion. Finely chop the white (about ¼ cup) and thinly slice the greens (about ⅓ cup), keeping them separate. Finely chop the bell pepper (about ½ cup).

In a large cast-iron skillet set on medium heat, melt the butter until it starts to bubble. Add the spring onion white and the bell pepper. Season with salt and pepper, and cook, stirring frequently, until tender, about 5 minutes. Add the corn kernels, season with salt and pepper, and cook, stirring constantly, until the corn is crisp-tender, about 2 minutes. Turn off the heat and stir in the spring onion greens, then immediately spoon the vegetables into a small bowl and set aside to cool completely.

To the mayonnaise mixture add the egg, parsley, 1¼ teaspoons salt, and several large grinds of black pepper and whisk until well combined. Add the cooled sautéed vegetables and the panko and stir again until well combined. Add the crabmeat and gently fold together until the mixture is well combined with a mix of both small and large pieces of crab. Refrigerate the crab cake mixture for 30 minutes. (This allows the panko to absorb some of the liquid, which will help the mixture firm up and make forming the cakes much easier.)

Scoop ½-cup portions of the crab cake mixture onto a large rimmed baking sheet and use your hands to lightly press each into a patty about 2½ inches wide; you should have 8 patties. (Alternatively, you can scoop ¼ cup portions to make 16 smaller patties.) Refrigerate the crab cakes while you heat the oil for frying.

Fit a wire rack into a large rimmed baking sheet or line a large plate with paper towels. Into a large cast-iron skillet set over medium heat, pour enough oil to cover the bottom by a scant ⅛ inch. When the oil immediately starts to sizzle as you sprinkle in a few panko crumbs, add half the crab cakes and cook until browned and crispy on the first side, 4 to

5 minutes (about 3 minutes for smaller cakes). Use a flat metal spatula to carefully flip each crab cake. Continue to cook until browned and crispy on the second side, 4 to 5 additional minutes (about 3 minutes for smaller cakes). If necessary, lower the heat so the crab cakes brown nicely but do not burn. When done, transfer the cakes to the rack and pan-fry the remaining cakes.

Place the crab cakes on a large serving platter and serve immediately, accompanied by the Peach Salsa.

"I consider myself a good friend of the crabs ... however, I cannot help but partake of their sweet meats when formed into cakes and drizzled with lemon." -ELLIOTT

PEACH SALSA

Makes 2 cups

2 medium-firm ripe large peaches

1 small shallot, finely diced

1 small jalapeño, finely diced

2 tablespoons fresh lime juice, plus more as needed

1 teaspoon honey, plus more as needed

Kosher salt

3 tablespoons coarsely chopped fresh cilantro leaves and soft stems

Peel the peaches (or leave unpeeled, if preferred), then halve and remove the pits. Finely dice the peaches and place in a medium bowl. Add the shallot, jalapeño, the 2 tablespoons of lime juice, the teaspoon of honey, and a large pinch of salt. Stir to combine, then fold in the cilantro. Taste for seasoning and add more lime juice, honey, or salt, if desired. Serve immediately or transfer to an airtight container and refrigerate for up to 3 days.

Fish Taco

WITH COLESLAW

FROM THE KITCHEN OF: **LINUS**

YIELD: **MAKES 4 SERVINGS**

The great thing about tacos is that you can make them with just about any ingredients you want! One of my favorite fillings is grilled chipotle tuna with homemade coleslaw. Don't worry; it's not as complicated as it sounds. All you have to do is mix up some spices and rub them on the tuna steaks along with some salt, then put the steaks on the grill for just a minute or so per side. While the steaks are still nice and hot, cut them into thin slices. Place a few slices into each tortilla, then add as much or as little of the coleslaw as you like. These tacos are a great companion on those long summer evenings fishing at the mountain lake. Something about the aroma seems to get the fish biting quicker! And you have to admit, it's fun to eat with your hands now and then.

INGREDIENTS

½ to ¾ teaspoon **CHIPOTLE POWDER**, as desired

¾ teaspoon **SMOKED PAPRIKA**

½ teaspoon **GROUND CUMIN**

½ teaspoon **GROUND CORIANDER**

2 (1-inch-thick) **TUNA STEAKS** (about 1 lb total)

KOSHER SALT

NEUTRAL HIGH-HEAT COOKING OIL, for the grill

8 (6-inch) **CORN TORTILLAS**

COLESLAW (recipe follows)

Sliced **RADISHES**

Coarsely chopped **FRESH CILANTRO LEAVES** and **SOFT STEMS**

HOT SAUCE and **LIME WEDGES**, for serving

In a small bowl, stir together the chipotle powder, smoked paprika, cumin, and coriander. Season the tuna steaks all over liberally with salt, then sprinkle the tops and bottoms of the tuna evenly with the spice mix. Use your hands to lightly rub the seasoning into the tuna, then place the steaks on a plate and chill in the refrigerator while you prepare the grill.

Preheat a charcoal or gas grill to medium-high heat. (Alternatively, use a large cast-iron grill pan set over medium-high heat on the stovetop.)

When the grill is hot, lightly brush the grates with oil. Place the tuna steaks on the grates and cook, turning once, until the tuna has deep grill marks and the fish is cooked to medium-rare or rare doneness, 1½ to 2 minutes per side. Transfer the tuna to a cutting board.

Clean off any spice rub left on the grates, then, working with 1 or 2 tortillas at a time, grill the tortillas until pliable and charred in spots, 30 seconds to 1 minute per side. Wrap the tortillas in a clean kitchen towel.

Thinly slice the tuna against the grain, then arrange the fish on the tortillas. Top with the Coleslaw, radishes, and cilantro. Serve immediately, with hot sauce and lime wedges on the side.

"Want to know the real reason we're closed on Wednesdays? I need my fish tacos once a week, but Pierre thinks the smell of fish would be bad for business!" –CAROLINE

COLESLAW

Makes about 4½ cups

4 cups lightly packed very thinly sliced red cabbage

4 cups lightly packed very thinly sliced savoy cabbage

1 medium carrot, grated on the large holes of a box grater (about ¾ cup)

¼ cup mayonnaise

3 tablespoons distilled white vinegar, plus more as needed

¾ teaspoon sugar

Kosher salt and freshly ground black pepper

¼ cup sliced scallions (green and white parts)

In a large bowl, combine the cabbages and carrots.

In a small bowl, whisk together the mayonnaise, vinegar, sugar, a large pinch of salt, and several large grinds of pepper. Pour the dressing over the vegetables and toss to coat. Season with additional salt, pepper, and vinegar, if needed. Let sit for 15 minutes at room temperature, then fold in the scallions and serve.

Fish Taco
with Coleslaw
80

Mango
Sticky Rice
84

Mango Sticky Rice

FROM THE KITCHEN OF: **LEO**

YIELD: **MAKES 4 TO 6 SERVINGS**

I love mangos! I could eat them for every meal and never get tired of them. But it's still nice to try eating them in different ways so they don't get boring. I had lots of mangos when I lived on the island—and coconuts, too.

Then my parrot family taught me a fancy dessert that uses sliced mangos and coconut milk with sweet rice. Just soak the rice all night so it gets nice and soft, cook it up, and stir in sweetened coconut milk. Top it with mango slices and it's ready to eat. The first time I made this, I just wanted to eat the mangos off the top, but it's all sweet and delicious. Get a little of everything in each spoonful!

INGREDIENTS

1 (13.5 to 14 oz) can **FULL-FAT COCONUT MILK**

½ to ⅔ cup **GRANULATED SUGAR**, as desired

KOSHER SALT

2 cups **THAI SWEET RICE** (sticky or glutinous rice), soaked for at least 4 hours and up to overnight

2 large or 4 small **RIPE ATAULFO** or **MANILA MANGOS**

TOASTED SESAME SEEDS or **COARSELY CHOPPED ROASTED SALTED CASHEWS**, for topping

Special Equipment
STEAMER INSERT and **LARGE POT**

CHEESECLOTH

In a medium saucepan over medium heat, combine the coconut milk, sugar, and ¾ teaspoon salt. Stir until the mixture is smooth, then simmer, stirring frequently and scraping down the sides of the saucepan occasionally, about 15 minutes. Remove from the heat, measure out ½ cup, and let cool at room temperature. Cover the saucepan with a lid.

Fill a large pot with 2 inches of water, cover with a tight-fitting lid, and bring to a boil over medium-high heat. Cut a large double layer of cheesecloth, wet it under cold water, squeeze out the excess water, then drape it inside a large steamer insert.

Drain the soaked rice and spread it evenly on the cheesecloth. Pull up the sides of the cheesecloth and tie in a knot at the top. Put the insert into the pot, cover again with the lid, and steam until the rice starts to plump up and get sticky, about 15 minutes. (To test, use a large spatula to lift up one side of the rice bundle; if the rice holds together in one piece, it is ready to flip. If the rice is still loose, steam it for 5 additional minutes.) When the rice is holding together, use a spatula (depending on the size of the spatula, you might need two to do this) to flip the rice bundle over and continue to steam until the rice is tender, translucent, and very sticky, 10 to 15 additional minutes. (The timing will vary depending on how long the rice was soaked for.)

Turn off the heat and use the spatula to transfer the wrapped rice to a large plate or baking sheet. Let cool enough so that it is safe to handle, then carefully untie or cut the cheesecloth and remove it from around the rice.

Add the warm sticky rice to the saucepan with the coconut milk and stir until well combined, but do not crush the grains. (The mixture will seem very saucy at this point, and that is okay.) Cover again with the lid and let sit until the rice has soaked up most of the coconut milk and the mixture is creamy and sticky, about 20 minutes, stirring once after 10 minutes.

Peel the mangos. Holding the mangos on edge, use a sharp knife to cut down on both sides of the pit, then cut along the pit to remove any remaining flesh. Score the mango pieces lengthwise into ¼-inch slices.

Divide the coconut sticky rice among 4 to 6 serving bowls or short glasses, then top with the sliced mangos. Drizzle with the reserved sweetened coconut milk, and sprinkle with the toasted sesame seeds or chopped cashews. Serve immediately.

"I like mine with extra mango!"
—LEO

Banana Pudding

FROM THE KITCHEN OF: **THE QUEEN OF SAUCE**

YIELD: **MAKES 4 SERVINGS** (see Queen's Tip)

Did you know that bananas are a tropical fruit? It's true! Luckily for us, we don't have to travel to any distant islands to enjoy this sweet treat. Here, we'll whip up a delicious pudding full of rich banana flavor using crème de banana along with sliced bananas, all layered with vanilla wafers. Then we can go all-out on the presentation, if you'd like, by topping each serving with brûléed banana halves. The contrast of crunchy caramelized sugar and smooth, creamy pudding is simply out of this world.

INGREDIENTS

3 cups **WHOLE MILK**

⅔ cup plus 1 tablespoon **GRANULATED SUGAR**

3½ tablespoons **CORNSTARCH**

KOSHER SALT

1⅓ cups **HEAVY CREAM**

3 **LARGE EGG YOLKS**, at room temperature

3 tablespoons (1½ fl oz) **CRÈME DE BANANA** (no higher than 30 percent alcohol)

1½ teaspoons **VANILLA EXTRACT**

2 tablespoons cold **UNSALTED BUTTER**, cut into cubes

2 tablespoons **CONFECTIONERS' SUGAR**

5 small **RIPE BANANAS**

70 miniature **VANILLA WAFERS**

Special Equipment
BUTANE COOKING TORCH (optional)

"Oh man, a nice big bowl of banana pudding has got to be the perfect way to cool down your mouth after a heaping helping of Spicy Eel! This is what Mom always makes for my birthday and I love it." –ABIGAIL

In a large saucepan over medium heat, warm the milk, stirring occasionally, until it just starts to steam, 6 to 8 minutes. Turn off the heat and leave the saucepan on the stove.

In a large bowl, whisk together ⅔ cup of the granulated sugar, the cornstarch, and ¼ teaspoon salt until well combined. Add ⅓ cup of the cream and the egg yolks, and whisk until smooth. Slowly whisk half the hot milk into the egg mixture until smooth. Then gradually whisk the egg-and-milk mixture into the milk in the saucepan. Turn the heat back on to medium and cook, whisking constantly, until the mixture starts to bubble, about 20 minutes. Be patient with this step and do not rush; the pudding needs to be cooked over moderate heat to ensure it doesn't scorch.

When the mixture starts to bubble, add the crème de banana and continue to cook, whisking constantly, until it has thickened to a pudding-like consistency, about 5 additional minutes. Remove from the heat and whisk in 1 teaspoon of the vanilla and the butter. Continue to whisk until the butter is melted, then spoon the pudding into a medium bowl. Place a piece of plastic wrap directly on top of the pudding and let cool at room temperature for 15 minutes. Transfer to the refrigerator to chill completely, about 2 hours.

In a medium bowl, combine ½ cup of the cream, 1 tablespoon of the confectioners' sugar, and ¼ teaspoon of the vanilla. Whisk vigorously until medium-stiff peaks form. Peel 4 of the bananas and thinly slice them on a slight bias, about ¼ inch thick. Divide them into 8 piles.

Spoon ¼ cup of the chilled pudding into the bottom of 4 large (16 oz) serving bowls, cups, or glasses (red wine glasses work particularly well), or into individual dessert dishes. Layer each with one batch of the banana slices, and 8 miniature vanilla wafers, then add another ¼ cup pudding, one-fourth of the whipped

Queen's Tip
If smaller servings are preferred, use 1-cup ramekins instead, and cut the final banana into 8 pieces for the brûlée effect.

cream, one batch of banana slices, and 8 more wafers. Divide the remaining pudding among the servings. Cover the puddings with plastic wrap and refrigerate at least 3 hours and up to overnight. (Test by inserting a long wooden skewer through the pudding; if there's no resistance, the wafers have softened.)

When you are ready to serve, combine the remaining ½ cup cream, remaining tablespoon confectioners' sugar, and remaining ¼ teaspoon vanilla in a medium bowl. Whisk vigorously until medium peaks.

Peel and cut the remaining banana in half lengthwise, then cut again in half crosswise to make 4 equal pieces. Scatter the remaining tablespoon sugar onto a small plate or oven-proof dish. Dip the cut side of each banana piece into the sugar until well coated. Carefully use a butane kitchen torch to caramelize the sugar or place under a broiler for a few minutes. Set the caramelized pieces aside until cooled and crispy, about 2 minutes.

Dollop the whipped cream on top of each banana pudding, then add a crisped banana piece to each serving. Coarsely crumble the remaining 6 vanilla wafers and sprinkle over the whipped cream. Serve immediately.

Pink Cake

YELLOW CAKE WITH A WATERMELON-STRAWBERRY JAM FILLING

FROM THE KITCHEN OF:	THE QUEEN OF SAUCE	YIELD: MAKES 10 TO 16 SERVINGS

Celebrate your next special summer occasion the Queen of Sauce way: with an absolutely outstanding pink cake! This sweet, luxurious cake is a feast for the eyes, as well as the taste buds, featuring the unmistakably summery flavor of strawberry and watermelon jelly between layers of soft, rich, velvety cake made with tangy buttermilk and fresh duck eggs. We'll jazz it up with a gorgeous pink cream cheese frosting that'll knock your socks off, and top it off with sweet-yet-tart freeze-dried strawberry hearts. A burst of creamy sweetness awaits in every forkful!

Don't worry if your strawberries don't come out looking like perfect little hearts; they'll still add plenty of color and flavor. Who's going to turn down such an appealing slice of cake just because the strawberries aren't quite heart-shaped? No one, that's who!

INGREDIENTS

Watermelon-Strawberry Jam

6 ounces (170 g) cubed **SEEDLESS WATERMELON**

⅓ cup (65 g) **GRANULATED SUGAR**

KOSHER SALT

6 ounces (170 g) **FRESH STRAWBERRIES**, hulled and finely chopped

2 teaspoons grated **FRESH LEMON ZEST**

2 tablespoons **CORNSTARCH**

3 tablespoons **WATER**

1½ tablespoons **FRESH LEMON JUICE**

Buttermilk Cake

1¼ cups (2½ sticks; 275 g) **UNSALTED BUTTER**, at room temperature, plus more for greasing

2½ cups (350 g) **ALL-PURPOSE FLOUR**

1¼ teaspoons **BAKING POWDER**

1¼ teaspoons **BAKING SODA**

KOSHER SALT

1½ cups (300 g) **GRANULATED SUGAR**

1 tablespoon **VANILLA BEAN PASTE** or **VANILLA EXTRACT**

2 **DUCK EGGS**, at room temperature

1½ cups (360 ml) **BUTTERMILK**, at room temperature

Strawberry-Cream Cheese Frosting

1⅛ ounces (33 g) **FREEZE-DRIED STRAWBERRIES** (about 1½ cups)

3¾ cups (453 g) **CONFECTIONERS' SUGAR** (one 1-pound box)

1 cup (2 sticks; 220 g) **UNSALTED BUTTER**, at room temperature

1 pound (450 g) **CREAM CHEESE**, at room temperature

Special Equipment

LARGE PIPING BAG (or **ZIPPERED PLASTIC BAG**) and **LARGE STAR TIP**

"Oh, my gosh, this cake is so good! It's so moist and sweet and fruity, and the strawberry hearts are adorable. I need to have one for my birthday, and one for Emily's birthday, and . . . and one for every Saturday!" –HALEY

FOR THE JAM: In a blender, blend the watermelon, granulated sugar, and a pinch of salt until smooth. Pour into a medium saucepan over medium heat, then stir in the strawberries and lemon zest, and simmer, stirring occasionally, until the strawberries soften and the jam turns a deep, dark red color, about 20 additional minutes, reducing the heat as needed to maintain the low simmer.

Whisk together the cornstarch and water and stir into the fruit mixture along with the lemon juice. Stir until smooth. The mixture will immediately thicken but continue to cook it, stirring frequently, until it bubbles and thickens to the consistency of thick fruit pie filling, about 4 minutes; you should no longer be able to taste the cornstarch. Transfer to a medium bowl and let cool at room temperature for 30 minutes. Then place in the refrigerator and chill until completely cooled and set, at least 2 hours and up to overnight.

FOR THE CAKE (SEE QUEEN'S TIP): Preheat the oven to 350°F (175°C). Generously grease 2 (9-inch; 23 cm) round cake pans with some butter, then line the bottoms with parchment paper. Grease the parchment paper with more butter.

"Yeah, what Haley said!" –JAS & VINCENT

Place a fine-mesh strainer over a medium bowl. In batches, spoon the flour, baking powder, and baking soda through the strainer into the bowl. Remove the strainer, add 1¼ teaspoons salt, and whisk until the mixture is well combined.

In a large bowl, beat the 1¼ cups (275 g) butter and the granulated sugar with an electric hand mixer on medium-high speed until pale and fluffy, about 5 minutes. Beat in the vanilla paste, then add the duck eggs, one at a time, and beat well after each. At low speed, mix in roughly one-third of the flour, followed by half the buttermilk. Follow with another third of the flour and the remaining buttermilk. Then add the remaining flour, mixing to ensure all ingredients are fully incorporated. Increase the speed to medium and mix until smooth. The batter will be thick.

Divide the batter between the 2 cake pans and smooth out the tops. Lightly drop each pan on a flat surface several times to help settle the batter and eliminate any air bubbles. Bake until the cakes are lightly golden on top and a cake tester or wooden pick inserted into the center comes out clean, about 35 minutes, rotating the cakes front to back once after 20 minutes.

Transfer the cakes to a wire rack and cool for 30 minutes. After 30 minutes, carefully invert them onto the rack, remove the parchment paper, and let cool completely.

FOR THE FROSTING: Place a fine-mesh strainer over a medium bowl. Set aside 8 small dried strawberries. In a spice grinder, working in batches, grind the remaining strawberries until they are a fine powder. Transfer to the strainer and use the back of a spoon or rubber spatula to push the powder through the strainer into the bowl (discard any seeds). Add the confectioners' sugar, then whisk to combine.

In a large bowl, beat together the butter and cream cheese with an electric hand mixer on medium-high speed until light and fluffy, about 2 minutes. With the mixer on low speed, add the strawberry powder, 1 cup (100 g) at a time, until the frosting is fairly smooth and creamy. Increase the mixer to medium-high and beat until the frosting is very smooth and slightly fluffy, about 2 minutes.

TO ASSEMBLE THE CAKE: Spread a couple spoonfuls of the frosting in the center of a large cake plate or cake stand to hold the cake in place, then add one cake layer, top side up.

Cut a 1-inch (2.5 cm) opening at the tip of a large piping bag and fill with 1 cup (190 g) of frosting. Pipe a thick line of frosting around the top edge of the cake so that the frosting is at least ½ inch (1.3 cm) wide. Then fill the inside of the frosting ring with the jam. Spread the jam in an even layer, making sure that it stays within the frosting border.

Squeeze any remaining frosting in the piping bag back into the bowl of frosting. Insert a large star piping tip into the piping bag (no need to clean the bag). Place the second cake layer on top of the first, then scoop 3 cups (570 g) of frosting onto the cake. Use an offset spatula to frost the top and sides of the cake, adding more frosting if needed (or removing some frosting if there is too much). Chill the cake in the refrigerator for 20 minutes. Fill the piping bag with the remaining frosting and chill the frosting as well.

Remove the cake and frosting from the refrigerator and pipe pink stars around the bottom and top edges of the cake. Decorate the top with the 8 reserved dried strawberries, then serve.

"Wow, the duck eggs really do make for a richer, fluffier cake. Maybe I should consider adding a few ducks to that coop that Shane set up for those blue chickens of his." **-MARNIE**

Blueberry Tart

FROM THE KITCHEN OF: PIERRE

YIELD: MAKES 8 TO 10 SERVINGS

You don't sell groceries for as long as I have without picking up a recipe or two. And it just so happens I've got a couple of really good summer dessert recipes hiding up my sleeve. Try this one on for size; I'm kind of famous around these parts for it. I can taste it already: a rustic cornmeal crust full of sweet blueberry curd (bonus points if you buy the blueberries from me, but I understand if you want to hand-pick from your own blueberry bushes . . . just don't even think about visiting JojaMart!), baked just long enough for the curd to set and then topped with fresh blueberries. You can dress it up with some vanilla bean ice cream if you're in a really decadent mood, or have a slice with a hot cup of coffee for a great summer breakfast.

INGREDIENTS

Cornmeal Crust

½ cup (1 stick; 110 g) **UNSALTED BUTTER**, at room temperature

¼ cup (50 g) **GRANULATED SUGAR**

1 **LARGE EGG YOLK**, at room temperature

1⅓ cups (185 g) **ALL-PURPOSE FLOUR**

⅓ cup (54 g) **FINELY GROUND YELLOW CORNMEAL**

KOSHER SALT

1½ tablespoons **WHOLE MILK**

Blueberry Curd

8 ounces (225 g) **FRESH BLUEBERRIES**, plus more for garnish

2 tablespoons **WATER**

½ cup (100 g) **GRANULATED SUGAR**

⅓ cup (80 ml) **FRESH LEMON JUICE** (from 2 small lemons)

1 tablespoon **CORNSTARCH**

KOSHER SALT

2 **LARGE EGGS**, at room temperature

2 **LARGE EGG YOLKS**, at room temperature

5 tablespoons (75 g) **COLD UNSALTED BUTTER**, cubed

¼ cup (75 g) **BLUEBERRY PRESERVES**

Special Equipment

One 9-inch (23 cm) **TART PAN** with removable bottom

FOR THE CORNMEAL CRUST: In a large bowl, combine the butter and sugar. Use an electric hand mixer on medium speed to blend until light and fluffy, about 3 minutes. Add the egg yolk and blend until smooth.

Add the flour, cornmeal, and ½ teaspoon salt and mix on low speed until combined and crumbly. Add the milk and mix until the dough starts to form large crumbles. The dough is ready when you can squeeze some of it in the palm of your hand and it holds together.

Use your hands to form the mixture into a mostly smooth dough, then transfer it to a 9-inch (23 cm) tart pan with a removable bottom. Press the dough evenly into the bottom and up the sides of the pan, getting it as close to ⅛ inch (3 mm) thick as possible. Use the bottom of a drinking glass or a measuring cup to help get the crust nice and even. Trim any excess dough from the edges of the tart pan. Prick the bottom of the crust all over with a fork, then chill in the refrigerator until firm, about 1 hour and up to overnight.

Set a baking sheet on the lowest rack of the oven and preheat the oven to 350°F (175°C). Line the tart crust with parchment paper or aluminum foil and fill to the very top of the crust with dry rice or dried beans.

Place the tart pan on the baking sheet and bake until the edges of the crust start to feel dry and set, 20 to 25 minutes. Carefully remove the parchment paper and the rice. Return the crust to the oven and continue to bake until the edges are golden brown and the dough is cooked through, about 15 minutes, rotating the baking sheet once after 8 minutes.

Remove the crust from the oven and cool completely on the baking sheet. Reduce the oven temperature to 325°F (165°C).

FOR THE BLUEBERRY CURD: In a large saucepan over medium heat, combine the 8 ounces (225 g) blueberries and the water and simmer until most of the blueberries have burst and released their juices, about 8 minutes, stirring occasionally and smashing some of the juicy berries against the side of the saucepan.

Strain the blueberry mixture through a fine-mesh strainer into a large glass bowl, pressing down on the berries to get every bit of juice out. Be sure to scrape off any pulp that is stuck to the back of the strainer; only the skin of the berries should be left in the strainer once you are done. Rinse out the strainer and place over a medium bowl. (You will use this later to strain the finished curd.)

Wash out the saucepan and fill it with 1 inch (2.5 cm) of water. Bring the water to a boil over medium-high heat, then lower the heat to medium (the water should be actively simmering).

To the glass bowl with the strained blueberry mixture add the sugar, ⅓ cup (80 ml) lemon juice, the cornstarch, and ¼ teaspoon salt. Whisk until smooth. Add the eggs and egg yolks and whisk again until smooth. Put the bowl on top of the saucepan of simmering water and cook, whisking constantly, until the mixture thickens to a consistency similar to a creamy berry milkshake, about 20 minutes. (Taste the curd to ensure that there is no longer any chalkiness from the cornstarch; if there is, continue to cook the curd for a couple additional minutes, then taste the curd again.)

Place the bowl on a kitchen towel or wipe the bottom of the bowl of any water and place it on a trivet, if possible. Slowly whisk in the butter, a couple of cubes at a time, whisking well after each addition, then whisk in the blueberry preserves until smooth. Strain the curd through the strainer into the bowl.

"Few things are more delicious than a dessert made from that first summer blueberry harvest; I'll admit that it's tough to bake on an open fire, so a slice of blueberry tart is an especially rare treat." **-LINUS**

FILL AND BAKE THE TART: Give the curd a good stir, then pour it into the cooled tart shell, spreading it into an even layer. Return the tart (still on the baking sheet) to the oven and bake until the top of the curd turns from shiny to matte and is slightly puffed and set around the edges but still slightly wobbly in the center, about 20 minutes, rotating the baking sheet once after 10 minutes.

Cool the tart on the hot baking sheet set over a wire rack for 1 hour, then transfer the tart to the refrigerator to cool completely, at least 2 hours and up to overnight.

SERVE THE TART: Garnish the tart with additional blueberries, remove the outer ring of the tart pan, and cut the tart into wedges.

Piña Colada

FROM THE KITCHEN OF: GUS

YIELD: **MAKES 4 SERVINGS**

When I try to imagine the perfect tropical drink, I can't come up with anything more fitting or iconic than the piña colada. I mean, it's got pineapple, it's got coconut, it's got rum—what could be more tropical than that? And it never ceases to amaze me how you can concoct such a delicious summer treat with just a few simple ingredients. It is equally delicious if you leave out the rum, so don't hesitate to serve it up however you'd like (see Queen's Tips).

For an extra-festive occasion, try serving these drinks in hollowed-out coconut shells. They're the perfect serving size, easy to hold, and sure to liven up the party.

INGREDIENTS

1 small ripe **PINEAPPLE** (about 3½ lb)

1 (13.5 to 14 oz) can **UNSWEETENED COCONUT CREAM**

⅔ cup **GRANULATED SUGAR**

KOSHER SALT

1½ cups good-quality **UNSWEETENED COCONUT WATER** (preferably fresh)

⅓ cup **FRESH LIME JUICE** (from about 3 limes)

⅔ cup (160 ml) **DARK RUM** (see Queen's Tips)

2 cups **ICE CUBES**

4 hollowed-out **COCONUT SHELLS** (optional)

RECIPE CONTINUES

On a cutting board, turn the pineapple on its side and use a sharp knife to cut off the top and bottom of the fruit. Stand the pineapple upright on the board and follow the natural shape of the fruit to cut away the rind. Use the knife to carefully cut away any brown "eyes" left behind. Quarter the pineapple lengthwise, then cut each quarter in half lengthwise again to create 8 long wedges. Cut away the core on each wedge, then slice the wedges crosswise into ½-inch pieces (about 6 cups total).

Spread the pineapple pieces on a large baking sheet and freeze until solid.

In a medium saucepan over medium heat, combine the coconut cream, sugar, and ¼ teaspoon salt. Whisk until the mixture is smooth. Bring the mixture to a gentle simmer, stirring frequently and scraping down the sides of the saucepan occasionally, and cook, adjusting the heat as needed, until reduced by about half (1 cup) and thickened to a

Queen's Tips

For a nonalcoholic version, add extra coconut water or your favorite tropical fruit juice in place of the rum.

Transfer any leftover cream of coconut to an airtight container and store in the refrigerator for up to 7 days. Let sit at room temperature for 20 to 30 minutes before using it. As the cream of coconut comes to room temperature, it might separate, but just give it a good stir and it will become smooth and creamy again.

consistency similar to maple syrup (the color will also go from milky white to a translucent grayish pink), 50 to 60 minutes. (Owing to its high fat content, the coconut cream might start to separate as it cooks down, but that is okay; keep stirring and the mixture will come back together.) Transfer the cream of coconut to a small bowl and let cool; it will thicken up significantly as it cools.

Add the frozen pineapple to a blender along with ½ cup of the cream of coconut (see Queen's Tips), the coconut water, lime juice, rum, and ice cubes. Blend until very smooth. (Depending on the size of your blender, you might have to do this in 2 batches.)

Pour the piña colada mixture into the coconut shells, if using (or into tall glasses). Garnish with a cocktail umbrella and a fun paper or reusable straw, and serve immediately.

"Ah, yeah . . . the feeling of sand on your feet, while sipping on a couple of piña coladas . . . now that's what I call a vacation. Just do yourself a favor and don't look at my toes, kid!" -PAM

FALL

Golden days of plenty

The coming of fall transforms the rolling green scenery of summer into a boundless landscape of shifting colors. As the heat of summer begins to subside, cool breezes become cold winds and leaves begin to fall. It's a time of change; some wild animals begin to store food away while others start preparing to hunker down for the long winter months. It's also a time of both visual and culinary beauty, as the first autumn chill brings with it an invitation to create masterpieces using a gourmet palette of vivid colors and flavors.

Fall is a time to celebrate the harvest—and to preserve it! For all you farmers out there, make sure to have your kegs and preserve jars ready to help make the bounty last all through winter. It's a real busy season, and I've got a cornucopia of dishes to keep you energized! Hearty soups, platters loaded with veritable rainbows of veggie goodness, and delectable sweets highlight the unique flavors of the season. One fall classic I know you'll love is my Salmon Dinner—if you can catch one! Or, maybe you're looking to power up before a long day out and about? Try a scrumptious vegetable-based Survival Burger or a colorful and tasty Super Meal, followed with a warm bowl of Blackberry Cobbler. Wash it all down with a sweet and refreshing glass of Cranberry Candy, and you'll be ready to take on anything the season can throw at you.

The days may be getting shorter, but that doesn't mean we have to curtail our culinary ambitions. In fact, I say we ought to take every opportunity to have ourselves a feast and make each one a meal to remember!

Radish Salad

FROM THE KITCHEN OF: **THE QUEEN OF SAUCE**

YIELD: **MAKES 4 TO 6 SERVINGS**

The crisp bite of a raw radish simply can't be beat. But there's definitely something to be said for the sweet-and-sour intensity of a pickled radish. So, why not combine the two to get the best of both worlds? A delicious plate chock-full of raw and pickled radishes, dressed with a simple vinaigrette using the pickling liquid and topped with fresh dill—I'm salivating just thinking about it! If you love radishes, this salad is bound to become one of your favorites; if not . . . well, this recipe may be just the thing to change your mind!

INGREDIENTS

1 pound (about 2 bunches) **RED RADISHES**, trimmed

3 tablespoons **GRANULATED SUGAR**

KOSHER SALT

1 teaspoon **BLACK PEPPERCORNS**

2 **BAY LEAVES**

¾ cup plus 1 tablespoon **WHITE WINE VINEGAR**

½ cup **WATER**

8 ounces (about 2 bunches) **FRENCH BREAKFAST RADISHES**, trimmed

1 tablespoon **DIJON MUSTARD**

2 teaspoons **HONEY**

FRESHLY GROUND BLACK PEPPER

¼ cup **EXTRA-VIRGIN OLIVE OIL**

⅓ cup hand-torn **FRESH DILL**

Set half the red radishes aside, then cut the remaining radishes into ½-inch wedges (about 2 heaping cups) and place in a medium bowl.

In a small saucepan, stir together the sugar, 2 teaspoons salt, the black peppercorns, the bay leaves, ¾ cup vinegar, and the water. Bring to a boil over medium-high heat and cook, stirring occasionally, until the sugar and salt have dissolved, about 3 minutes.

Pour the hot vinegar mixture over the radishes in the bowl and stir to combine. Let cool completely, about 1 hour. Transfer to the refrigerator to chill.

When ready to serve, very thinly slice the remaining red radishes (about 2 cups), halve or quarter the breakfast radishes (depending on their size, about 2 cups), and place both in a large bowl. Use a fork or small slotted spoon to remove the pickled radishes from the pickling liquid (leave behind the bay leaves and peppercorns) and add to the large bowl.

Measure out ¼ cup of the pickling liquid and place in a medium bowl. Add the remaining tablespoon of vinegar, the mustard, and honey. Season with salt and pepper, then whisk to combine. Continue to whisk vigorously while slowly streaming in the olive oil to make a vinaigrette.

Drizzle the vinaigrette over the radishes in the large bowl, season with salt and pepper, and gently toss to combine. Sprinkle with most of the dill, saving a few pieces for garnish, and fold to combine. Transfer the radishes to a serving platter or bowl, garnish with the reserved dill, and serve.

Autumn's Bounty, Vegetable Medley, and Red Plate

ROASTED VEGETABLE GRAZING BOARD WITH DIPS

FROM THE KITCHEN OF: **THE QUEEN OF SAUCE**

YIELD: **MAKES 8 TO 12 SERVINGS**

Here's a question I hear all the time: "What can I do with roasted vegetables?" And the answer to that question is another question: What can't you do with roasted vegetables? Let me give you just a few examples. We'll roast up a plethora of fall veggies and then make a creamy sweet potato and pumpkin dip, a sweet and tangy tomato and beet medley, and a gorgeous batch of cheesy cabbage wedges. Once everything's ready, we'll arrange it all artistically on a grazing board, turning the whole thing into a veritable buffet!

It'll be a feast of fall flavors, an irresistible platter of colorful roasted veggies, dips, and other fall delicacies. And don't sweat it if you don't have a suitable board for the arrangement; you can always use a platter or a large plate or two instead. Everything will be just as delicious!

Autumn's Bounty

AUTUMN'S BOUNTY
Smoky Sweet Potato and Pumpkin Dip

8 ounces **SWEET POTATO**, peeled and cut into ¾-inch cubes

8 ounces **EDIBLE PUMPKIN**, such as Long Island cheese pumpkin or Cinderella pumpkin, peeled and cut into ¾-inch cubes

½ large **YELLOW ONION**, coarsely chopped

3 **GARLIC CLOVES**, unpeeled

¼ cup **EXTRA-VIRGIN OLIVE OIL**, plus more for drizzling

¾ teaspoon **SMOKED PAPRIKA**, plus more for sprinkling

½ teaspoon **GROUND CUMIN**

KOSHER SALT and **FRESHLY GROUND BLACK PEPPER**

⅓ cup **PLAIN FULL-FAT GREEK YOGURT**

¼ cup **TAHINI**

2 tablespoons **WATER**, plus more as needed

1½ tablespoons **APPLE CIDER VINEGAR**

⅓ cup coarsely chopped **SMOKED ALMONDS**

POMEGRANATE SEEDS (arils), for garnish

VEGETABLE MEDLEY
Spicy Roasted Cherry Tomatoes and Olives; Sweet-and-Sour Roasted Golden Beets

6 **GARLIC CLOVES**

6 tablespoons plus 2 teaspoons **EXTRA-VIRGIN OLIVE OIL**

½ cup pitted **CASTELVETRANO OLIVES**, torn in half or thirds

2 long strips of **LEMON ZEST**

2 long strips of **ORANGE ZEST**

2 large **FRESH THYME SPRIGS**

12 ounces **CHERRY TOMATOES** on the vine

¼ to ½ teaspoon **RED PEPPER FLAKES**

KOSHER SALT

3 tablespoons **WHITE WINE VINEGAR**

3 tablespoons **WATER**

1 teaspoon **CORIANDER SEEDS**, lightly crushed

FRESHLY GROUND BLACK PEPPER

12 ounces **GOLDEN BEETS**, peeled and cut into ½-inch wedges

½ to ¾ teaspoon **HONEY**

1 cup lightly packed coarsely chopped **LEAFY BEET GREENS**

RED PLATE
Roasted Red Cabbage with White Miso Cheese Sauce and Nori; Radishes with Honey-Miso Butter

1 small **RED CABBAGE** (about 1½ lb), cut into 1-inch wedges, with the core intact

3 tablespoons **TOASTED SESAME OIL**

KOSHER SALT and **FRESHLY GROUND BLACK PEPPER**

10 tablespoons **BUTTER** (1 stick + 2 tablespoons), at room temperature

2½ tablespoons **ALL-PURPOSE FLOUR**

1 cup **WHOLE MILK**, at room temperature

4 ounces **FONTINA CHEESE**, grated

3½ tablespoons **WHITE MISO PASTE**

2 teaspoons **HONEY**

2 tablespoons thinly sliced **SCALLIONS** (white and green parts)

2 small roasted **SEAWEED SNACK SHEETS**, cut into thin bite-size strips, for garnish

2 bunches **RED** or **BREAKFAST RADISHES** (or mix) with leafy green tops

---

Suggested Accompaniments

FALL CHICORY, such as curly endive or treviso

FRESH VEGETABLES, such as small rainbow carrots, sliced cucumbers

Grilled or toasted **PITA BREAD**

Toasted slices of **BREAD** (page 58)

Assorted **CRACKERS**

Vegetable Medley

MAKE THE AUTUMN'S BOUNTY: Preheat the oven to 375°F.

In a 9 by 13-inch baking dish, combine the sweet potato, pumpkin, onion, garlic, 2 tablespoons of the olive oil, the smoked paprika, and cumin. Season liberally with salt and pepper, and bake until the vegetables are very tender and browned in spots, 50 to 60 minutes, stirring several times. (If at any point, the vegetables start to become too dark before tender, stir in a splash or two of water.) Remove from the oven and let the vegetables cool.

Squeeze the garlic from their skins and put in a food processor along with the other roasted vegetables. Add the remaining 2 tablespoons olive oil, the yogurt, tahini, 2 tablespoons water, the apple cider vinegar, and almonds. Blend until smooth, scraping down the side of the processor bowl; adjust the consistency with additional water if needed, and season with salt and pepper.

Transfer the dip to a serving bowl, drizzle with additional olive oil, sprinkle with additional smoked paprika, and garnish with the pomegranate seeds.

MAKE THE VEGETABLE MEDLEY: Preheat the oven to 375°F.

Thinly slice 2 of the garlic cloves and place in a small bowl. In a glass pie plate, arrange the remaining 4 garlic cloves, the olives, lemon zest, orange zest, and thyme in a single layer. Top with the cherry tomatoes on the vine. Drizzle with 4 tablespoons of the olive oil, and season with the red pepper flakes and salt.

In a 2-quart baking dish, stir together the vinegar, water, 2 tablespoons of olive oil, the coriander seeds, a large pinch of salt, and several grinds of black pepper. Add the beets and gently stir to coat with the liquid. Cover the baking dish with aluminum foil, and place both the beets and the cherry tomatoes in the oven.

Bake the cherry tomatoes until tender and some of the tomatoes are starting to split, about 30 minutes. Remove the tomatoes and let cool.

Remove the foil from the beets and give them a good stir, then continue to cook until the beets are fork-tender and the cooking liquid has reduced slightly, about 30 additional minutes, stirring the beets a couple of times while they cook. Remove the beets from the oven and stir in ½ teaspoon of the honey. Taste one of the beet wedges; it should be a mix of sweet and sour. Add the remaining ¼ teaspoon of honey if you prefer them even sweeter. Set aside to cool slightly.

In a medium cast-iron skillet over medium heat, warm the remaining 2 teaspoons olive oil. Add the sliced garlic and cook, stirring frequently, until tender, 2 to 3 minutes. Add the beet greens, season lightly with salt and pepper, and cook, stirring occasionally, until wilted and just tender, about 1 minute. Stir the sautéed beet greens into the roasted beets.

In a small bowl, combine the remaining ½ cup butter, the remaining 2 tablespoons of miso paste, the honey, and several large grinds of black pepper. Stir until smooth and slightly fluffy. Taste for seasoning and add salt and pepper if needed, then stir in the scallions. Transfer to a small serving bowl or ramekin.

ASSEMBLE THE GRAZING BOARD: Arrange the sweet potato and pumpkin dip, the honey-miso butter, the roasted tomatoes, and the roasted beets on an extra-large wooden cutting board. (Alternatively, place everything on a couple of long pieces of butcher paper.) Arrange the roasted red cabbage in a corner of the board (or small platter, if you are using butcher paper), then drizzle with the cheese sauce and sprinkle with the nori strips. Spoon any remaining sauce into a small bowl and serve it alongside the cabbage.

Arrange the radishes around the honey-miso butter, then fill the rest of the cutting board with any or all of the suggested accompaniments.

Both roasted vegetables can be served directly in their baking dishes, but you can also transfer them to serving dishes, if you prefer.

MAKE THE RED PLATE: Preheat the oven to 400°F. Line a baking sheet with parchment paper.

Arrange the cabbage wedges in a single layer on the baking sheet; then brush on all sides with the sesame oil and season with salt and pepper. Roast until the cabbage is tender and some of the leaves are crisp, about 20 minutes.

In a medium saucepan, melt 2 tablespoons of the butter. Add the flour and cook, whisking constantly to break up any clumps, for 2 minutes. Whisk in the milk until the mixture is smooth, then switch to a rubber spatula and stir constantly until the mixture thickens and just starts to faintly bubble, 6 to 8 minutes. Allow the mixture to continue to bubble for 2 minutes; the consistency will be similar to really thick pudding.

Remove the saucepan from the heat and stir in the cheese, 1½ tablespoons of the miso paste, and several large grinds of black pepper. Continue to stir until the cheese is melted and the sauce is smooth. Cover with a lid to keep the cheese sauce warm.

Red Plate

Autumn's Bounty,
Vegetable Medley,
and Red Plate
104

Pumpkin
Soup
110

Pumpkin Soup

WITH PECORINO FRICO

FROM THE KITCHEN OF: ROBIN	YIELD: **MAKES 4 TO 6 SERVINGS**

I remember spending fall days as a kid at my grandma's house, climbing trees and playing in her pumpkin patch until she called me in. She'd have me pick out a couple of pumpkins on my way back, which she would roast in preparation for her famous Pumpkin Soup. Everything was made from scratch, from the stock to the pumpkin puree, and I could taste the love that went into every spoonful. As I got older, she let me help, and she finally taught me the whole recipe once she decided I was ready.

She used to say it stuck to your ribs and kept you warm and tough through the winter. I don't know about all that, but I've made a sort of good-luck tradition out of cooking a big pot of this Pumpkin Soup a couple of times every year, including for Sebby's birthday. He'd never admit it, but I'm pretty sure he loves the stuff! I've come up with my own deluxe addition, though: I top each bowl with oven-toasted cheese crisps. They add a nice salty crunch that rounds out the flavors of the soup perfectly.

INGREDIENTS

1 small **KABOCHA SQUASH** (about 2½ lb)

3 tablespoons **EXTRA-VIRGIN OLIVE OIL**

KOSHER SALT and **FRESHLY GROUND BLACK PEPPER**

2 tablespoons **UNSALTED BUTTER**

1 large **YELLOW ONION**, thinly sliced

3 **GARLIC CLOVES**, sliced

1 (1-inch) piece of **FRESH GINGER**, peeled and finely chopped

½ cup **APPLE CIDER**

1½ tablespoons **APPLE CIDER VINEGAR**

1 large branch **FRESH THYME**

1 **FRESH ROSEMARY SPRIG**

2 **BAY LEAVES**

6 cups **VEGETABLE STOCK** (page 25)

⅓ cup **SOUR CREAM**

3 to 5 teaspoons **WHOLE MILK**

PECORINO FRICO (recipe follows), coarsely crumbled, for garnish

Preheat the oven to 400°F. Line a baking sheet with parchment paper.

Lay the squash on its side and carefully cut off the part of the top that has the stem. Sit the squash upright and slice it in half from the top to the sturdy bottom. Remove the knife from the squash and use your hands to crack it in half. Use a spoon to remove the seeds and scrape out as much of the stringy innards as possible. Carefully cut out the bottom of the squash. Cut each squash half in half again (4 pieces total). Peel the squash and cut it into 1-inch cubes. (They do not have to be perfect, but all of the pieces should be about the same size.)

Transfer the squash to a large bowl, drizzle with the olive oil, season liberally with salt and pepper, and toss to coat. Arrange the squash in a single layer on the baking sheet. Bake until browned in spots and very tender, 35 to 40 minutes, stirring the squash once after 20 minutes.

In a large Dutch oven over medium heat, melt the butter. When the butter starts to bubble, add the onion, season with salt and pepper, and cook, stirring occasionally, until softened, 12 to 15 minutes. Add the garlic and ginger and cook, stirring constantly, until softened, 2 to 4 minutes. Increase the heat to medium-high and add the cider, vinegar, thyme, rosemary, and bay leaves and cook at a low boil until the liquid has reduced almost completely, about 5 minutes. Add 5 cups of the stock and the roasted squash, and bring to a boil. Reduce the heat to medium, cover partially with a lid, and cook for 30 minutes. Remove the bay leaves, thyme, and rosemary and transfer the soup to a blender. (Depending on the size of your blender, this might have to be done in batches.) Remove the blender cap and place a kitchen towel over the opening. (This will allow steam to escape during the blending process.) Blend the soup until very smooth, then pour it back into the Dutch oven. (Alternatively, you can use an immersion blender to puree the soup.) Adjust the thickness of the soup with the remaining stock, if desired. Season with additional salt and pepper, if needed, then bring the soup to a simmer over medium heat, 10 to 15 minutes, stirring occasionally.

Meanwhile, in a small bowl, stir together the sour cream, 3 teaspoons of milk, and several large grinds of black pepper. The sour cream should drizzle off a spoon in thick ribbons. Whisk in the remaining 2 teaspoons milk, if needed, ½ teaspoon at a time until you reach that consistency. Season to taste with salt.

Ladle the hot soup into serving bowls, drizzle with some of the sour cream, and garnish with the Pecorino Frico. Serve immediately.

Queen's Tip

If you're attending this year's Fall Fair, don't forget to replenish! Here's a meal tip for you so you don't go hungry: Start with Pumpkin Soup (page 110), followed by Salmon Dinner (page 130), and a tasty slice of Blackberry Cobbler (page 134).

PECORINO FRICO

Makes about 12 frico

½ cup finely grated pecorino romano cheese

2 tablespoons raw pepitas

Place racks in the upper and lower thirds of the oven and preheat the oven to 375°F. Line 2 baking sheets with parchment paper or silicone mats.

In a small bowl, stir together the cheese and pepitas. Spoon a scant tablespoon of the cheese mixture onto one of the baking sheets and lightly pat into a 3-inch round. Repeat with the remaining cheese mixture to make 5 more rounds, spacing the rounds at least 1 inch apart on the baking sheet. Repeat with remaining cheese mixture, using the other baking sheet. Bake until the cheese is completely melted and lightly browned in spots, 7 to 9 minutes, rotating the baking sheets top to bottom and front to back after 4 minutes.

Let the rounds cool on the baking sheets for 2 minutes, then use a flat spatula to carefully transfer them to a wire rack to cool completely. The frico will crisp up as they cool. Store in an airtight container at room temperature for up to 3 days.

"Don't tell my mom I said this, but her pumpkin soup is my favorite thing about fall by far."

—SEBASTIAN

Shrimp Stock

FROM THE KITCHEN OF: THE QUEEN OF SAUCE

YIELD: MAKES 2 CUPS

As delicious and as adaptable as a good vegetable stock can be, there are still some dishes that need a little something different. A number of seafood recipes, for example, would fare much better with a stock made from, you know, seafood! Well, it just so happens that I have the perfect solution: a seafood stock made from shrimp shells! It's just as easy to prepare as my Vegetable Stock (page 25), requiring only shrimp shells, water, and aromatics, and it'll give your seafood dishes that extra oomph that'll have everyone singing your culinary praises.

INGREDIENTS

SHRIMP SHELLS from 1 pound fresh shrimp

1 small **YELLOW ONION**, quartered

1 tablespoon **BLACK PEPPERCORNS**

4 **GARLIC CLOVES,** smashed

2 cups **WATER**

In a medium saucepan over medium-high heat, combine the shrimp shells, onion, black peppercorns, and garlic. Cook, stirring constantly, until the shells turn bright orangey-red, about 3 minutes. Add the water and bring to a boil, then reduce to low, cover with a lid, and simmer for 30 minutes.

Pour the stock through a fine-mesh strainer set over a large bowl, pressing down on the shells to extract as much flavor as possible. Discard the solids. Use immediately, or let the stock cool completely and then transfer to an airtight container. Store in the refrigerator for up to 3 days or in the freezer for up to 3 months.

"Using this stock in Fish Stew is only the tip of the iceberg, sweetie. Try substituting it for other stocks, and you can give just about any dish a burst of seafood flavor." -SANDY

Fish Stew

MIXED SEAFOOD IN A ROASTED TOMATO BROTH

FROM THE KITCHEN OF: **WILLY**

YIELD: **MAKES 4 TO 6 SERVINGS**

Aye, the sea . . . she's as temperamental as a bonnie lass. Some days the lines come up empty, while on others the waters are overflowing with splashing fish. This here's a good recipe for times when you've got more seafood than you know what to do with. This soup starts with tomatoes and seafood stock—the perfect marriage o'land and sea. And with all those nice big pieces of fish and other seafood, every spoonful's guaranteed to be a fisherman's feast!

If you can't get your hands on any periwinkle snails, you can use clams or shrimp instead and it'll be almost as good. Oh, and don't forget to serve yourself up a warm, toasty piece of bread on the side; you'll definitely be wanting something to mop up every last drop from the bowl.

INGREDIENTS

1 pound **RAINBOW CHERRY TOMATOES**, halved

3½ tablespoons **EXTRA-VIRGIN OLIVE OIL**, plus more for drizzling

KOSHER SALT

4 cups **SHRIMP STOCK** (page 113) or store-bought fish or seafood stock

1 large ripe **BEEFSTEAK TOMATO**

2 large **SHALLOTS**, chopped

4 **GARLIC CLOVES**, minced

1 small **RED BELL PEPPER**, cored, seeded, and thinly sliced

¼ to ½ teaspoon **RED PEPPER FLAKES**, plus more as needed

1½ cups (12 fl oz) **DRY WHITE WINE**

1 pound **STEELHEAD TROUT** (or salmon), cleaned, skin removed, cut into 2-inch pieces

8 live **CRAYFISH** or fresh large head-on, shell-on **SHRIMP**

12 ounces large **PERIWINKLE SNAILS** or **LITTLENECK CLAMS**, rinsed well and scrubbed clean

12 ounces **MUSSELS**, any beards removed, scrubbed clean

Whole **FRESH FLAT-LEAF PARSLEY LEAVES**, for garnish

Lightly toasted slices of **BREAD** (page 58), for serving

RECIPE CONTINUES

Preheat the oven to 375°F. Line a baking sheet with parchment paper.

Spread the cherry tomatoes on the baking sheet and drizzle with 1½ tablespoons of the olive oil; stir to coat with the oil. Season liberally with salt, then flip all the tomatoes so they are cut side up. Roast in the oven until tender and the skins are shriveled and lightly browned on the bottom, about 45 minutes. Let cool completely.

Place the cooled tomatoes in a blender, add the stock, and blend until smooth.

Cut the beefsteak tomato in half. Put a box grater in a shallow bowl and grate the cut sides of the tomato on the large holes of the grater. The flesh will fall into the bowl and you will be left with just the tomato skin (which you can save to make Vegetable Stock, page 25).

In a small Dutch oven, warm the remaining 2 tablespoons olive oil on medium heat. Add the shallots, season with salt, and cook, stirring occasionally, until tender, about 10 minutes. Add the garlic, red bell pepper, and red pepper flakes and cook, stirring frequently, until the

bell pepper is just starting to soften, about 3 minutes. Stir in the grated tomato and the wine, increase the heat to medium-high, and cook until reduced by half, about 10 minutes. Add the tomato-stock mixture and bring to a low boil, about 10 minutes.

Season the trout with salt. Then add to the simmering broth, cover, and cook until the fish is opaque and just cooked through, 2 to 3 minutes. Use a slotted spoon to transfer the fish to a plate. Add the crayfish or shrimp, cover, and cook until the crayfish shells turn bright red (or the shrimp go from translucent to opaque), 4 to 6 minutes (or 3 to 5 minutes for the shrimp). Use tongs to remove to a large bowl. Add the periwinkle snails or clams, cover, and cook the snails for 5 to 7 minutes (they will not change appearance when cooked, so timing depends on the size of the snails), or cook the clams until they just open, 3 to 5 minutes. Remove to the same bowl as the crayfish or shrimp. Add the mussels, cover, and cook until they just open, 2 to 4 minutes.

Add the cooked shellfish back to the Dutch oven and stir gently to combine. Season the broth with additional salt, if needed, then nestle the fish evenly in the hot broth.

To serve, ladle the fish stew into serving bowls, drizzle with additional olive oil, and sprinkle with the parsley leaves. Serve immediately, accompanied by the toast.

"This scent . . . it reminds me of my days at sea, sailing with my husband. We'd make big pots of seafood soup every time we managed to find tomatoes at some port or another. *sniff* To think I'd almost forgotten . . ." —BIRDIE

Bean Hotpot

SWEET-AND-SOUR BEAN CASSEROLE

FROM THE KITCHEN OF: **CLINT**

YIELD: **MAKES 4 SERVINGS**

I like this recipe; after I eat it, the metal I'm working on always seems to bend to my will. Plus, it gives me the stamina to stand up to the heat of the furnace all day. Just mix up a sweet-and-sour sauce, combine it with beans and mushrooms, and divide it into ramekins. Top each one with some sliced potatoes and butter, and bake them to a golden brown. I usually put mine into the blast furnace, but I guess most people probably just have an oven at home. You can eat them right out of the dishes they're baked in, so there aren't as many dishes to wash afterwards.

The recipe makes four individual portions, so you can have one right away and refrigerate the rest for later. Or, you know, share with your family and friends.

INGREDIENTS

¾ cup dried large **LIMA BEANS**, soaked overnight (see Queen's Tip)

¾ cup dried **RED KIDNEY BEANS**, soaked overnight (see Queen's Tip)

KOSHER SALT

1 small **FRESH ROSEMARY SPRIG**

8 ounces **GREEN BEANS**, trimmed and cut into 1-inch pieces

3 tablespoons **EXTRA-VIRGIN OLIVE OIL**

8 ounces **CREMINI MUSHROOMS**, thinly sliced

FRESHLY GROUND BLACK PEPPER

2 large **SHALLOTS**, chopped

3 **GARLIC CLOVES**, minced

12 ounces **CHERRY TOMATOES**, quartered

1½ teaspoons chopped **FRESH THYME LEAVES**

3 tablespoons **APPLE CIDER VINEGAR**

3 tablespoons packed **DARK BROWN SUGAR**

1 tablespoon **WORCESTERSHIRE SAUCE**

½ cup **VEGETABLE STOCK** (page 25)

1 small **RUSSET POTATO** (about 4 oz), very thinly sliced

2 tablespoons **UNSALTED BUTTER**, melted

¼ cup thinly sliced **SCALLIONS** (white and green parts)

Special Equipment
4 (1½ cup; 12-ounce) **OVEN-SAFE RAMEKINS**

Drain the lima beans and kidney beans, and rinse well. Place the beans in a large pot over medium heat, cover with 2 inches of water, and bring to a boil. Lower the heat and simmer the beans, uncovered, for 20 minutes, skimming off any foam that floats to the top. Stir in a large pinch of salt and add the rosemary sprig, then continue to simmer the beans, adjusting the heat and adding more water as needed to keep them covered, until the beans are tender but not mushy, 1 to 1½ additional hours, stirring occasionally.

Discard the rosemary, and drain the beans well. Pick out any loose rosemary leaves, if desired. Place the beans in a large bowl, and cover with a damp paper towel.

Clean out the pot, fill halfway with water, and bring to a boil over medium-high heat. Fill a medium bowl with ice water and season the water aggressively with salt. Line a large plate with paper towels.

When the water is boiling, season it aggressively with salt and add the green beans. Cook, stirring occasionally, until the beans turn bright green, about 30 seconds. The beans will still be crisp at this point. Use a slotted spoon to transfer them to the ice bath and stir several times until they are no longer hot. Transfer to the paper-towel-lined plate to cool.

Preheat the oven to 375°F.

In a large Dutch oven or high-sided skillet over medium-high heat, warm 2 tablespoons of the olive oil. Add the mushrooms and cook, stirring occasionally, until tender and well browned in spots, about 10 minutes. Season with salt and pepper, then transfer to a bowl to cool.

Reduce the heat to medium and add the remaining tablespoon of olive oil. Add the shallots, season with salt and pepper, and cook, stirring frequently, until softened, 8 to 10 minutes. Add the garlic and cook until softened, about 2 minutes more. Drop the tomatoes and thyme into the pot; then add the vinegar, brown sugar, and Worcestershire sauce. Stir to combine, increase the heat slightly, and simmer, stirring occasionally, until the tomatoes are almost all broken down and the mixture forms a loose sauce with a concentrated sweet-and-sour flavor, about 10 minutes. Stir in the lima and kidney beans, mushrooms, and the stock and bring back to a simmer, about 5 minutes. Turn off the heat, stir in the green beans, and season to taste with salt and pepper.

Divide the bean mixture among 4 large oven-safe ramekins (about 1½ cups of mixture per ramekin). In a medium bowl, combine the potato slices, melted butter, and a large pinch of salt and pepper. Toss to combine, then arrange the slices in overlapping single layers on top of the bean mixture in each ramekin.

Queen's Tip

If you want to skip cooking the beans from scratch, use 3 cups (about 1 lb) of rinsed and drained canned beans instead.

Place the ramekins onto a rimmed baking sheet, cover the ramekins with aluminum foil, and bake for 30 minutes. Remove the foil, return the ramekins to the oven, and continue to bake until the potatoes are tender, have become golden brown in spots, and are crispy around the edges (the bean mixture should also be bubbling away by this point), about 30 additional minutes.

Let the bean hotpots rest for 5 minutes, then garnish with the scallions and serve.

"It's so flavorful, yet so nutritious; I almost feel like it's violating the laws of nature in some way! Did you know that green beans are actually fruits, botanically speaking?"

-DEMETRIUS

Survival Burger

EGGPLANT AND BEAN PATTIES WITH PICKLED CARROT RIBBONS

FROM THE KITCHEN OF: **LINUS**

YIELD: **MAKES 4 SERVINGS**

If you spend all your time outdoors, you'll end up learning a thing or two about living off the land. Sometimes you have to be creative with what nature has to offer. This recipe does just that. It's a special type of burger that is well loved by foragers, woodcutters, and adventurers of all kinds. The patty is made from eggplant, beans, and wonderful herbs, and it is satisfying and delicious on those long expeditions into the deep forest. I suggest using a sesame brioche bun. (I have a spot where I find them, but it's secret.) Top the patty with pickled cave carrots and a special sauce, and I think you'll be very, very happy.

INGREDIENTS

Burger Sauce

⅓ cup **MAYONNAISE**

⅓ cup **KETCHUP**

2 tablespoons **YELLOW MUSTARD**

3 tablespoons finely chopped **DILL PICKLE CHIPS**

2 tablespoons finely chopped **SHALLOTS**

KOSHER SALT

Survival Burger Patties

1 small **EGGPLANT** (about 12 oz), cut into 1-inch pieces

1 large **SHALLOT**, peeled and quartered

4 **GARLIC CLOVES**, unpeeled

3 tablespoons **EXTRA-VIRGIN OLIVE OIL**

KOSHER SALT and **FRESHLY GROUND BLACK PEPPER**

1 **LARGE EGG**

½ cup **PANKO**

½ teaspoon **SMOKED PAPRIKA**

½ teaspoon **GROUND CUMIN**

¾ cup canned **CANNELLINI BEANS**, rinsed and drained well (or homemade canned; see Queen's Tip)

¾ cup cooked and cooled **WILD RICE** (see Queen's Tip)

3 tablespoons **NEUTRAL HIGH-HEAT COOKING OIL, TALLOW**, or **LARD**, for frying

4 slices **SHARP WHITE CHEDDAR CHEESE**

Assembly

4 **SESAME SEED BRIOCHE-STYLE HAMBURGER BUNS**, split and lightly toasted

4 large pieces jarred **ROASTED RED BELL PEPPERS**, drained well (optional)

PICKLED CARROT RIBBONS (recipe follows)

4 **LETTUCE LEAVES**

FOR THE BURGER SAUCE: In a small bowl, stir together the mayonnaise, ketchup, mustard, pickles, and shallots. Season with salt and refrigerate until ready to use.

MAKE THE PATTIES: Preheat the oven to 400°F. Line a large baking sheet with parchment paper. Line a small baking sheet with parchment as well.

Place the eggplant, shallot, and garlic on the large baking sheet. Drizzle with the olive oil and season liberally with salt and pepper. Bake until the vegetables are tender and golden brown in spots, 35 to 40 minutes, stirring several times to ensure even browning. Let the mixture cool for 20 minutes.

In a large bowl, whisk the egg until smooth, then stir in the panko.

Squeeze the roasted garlic out of the skins (discard the skins), then add the garlic, eggplant, and shallot to the bowl of a food processor. Sprinkle in the smoked paprika and cumin. Process until the mixture is partially smooth but still fairly chunky. Add the beans and wild rice, and pulse several times until just combined. Taste and season with salt and pepper, as needed.

Add the blended vegetable mixture to the panko mixture and use a rubber spatula or your hands to mix until well combined. Divide the mixture into 4 portions (about ½ cup each) and shape into ½-inch thick patties that are roughly 3½ inches (8.8 cm) in diameter. Arrange the patties in a single layer on the small baking sheet and place in the freezer until the patties are dry to the touch and firm enough to pick up comfortably with your hands or a spatula, about 30 minutes. (You want the patties to be partially frozen on the outside but not rock-hard. If making ahead, you can fully freeze the patties, then let them thaw at room temperature for 30 minutes before cooking them.)

RECIPE CONTINUES

Queen's Tip

Have fun with this burger recipe and make it your own by swapping out the cannellini beans for your favorite beans (black beans or red kidney beans work really well) and the wild rice for your favorite starchy grain, such as brown rice or farro.

Place a large cast-iron skillet on medium heat. When the skillet is hot, pour in the cooking oil and swirl to coat. Add the patties and cook until deeply browned, with a crispy crust on both sides, about 5 minutes per side. (If the patties brown too quickly before they are heated through, turn down the heat slightly.) Turn the heat off and lay a slice of white cheddar cheese on each patty, cover the skillet with a lid, and let the cheese melt in the residual heat, about 2 minutes.

TO ASSEMBLE THE BURGER: Spread some of the burger sauce on the toasted bottoms of the buns and top each with a patty. Add a piece of roasted pepper (if using) and a good forkful of the carrot ribbons. Top with a lettuce leaf. Spread some burger sauce on the bun tops and place on top of the lettuce. Serve immediately.

PICKLED CARROT RIBBONS

Makes about 2 cups, including brine

2 medium purple carrots (about 6 oz), peeled

¾ cup Concord grape juice

½ cup distilled white vinegar

1 tablespoon granulated sugar

Kosher salt

1 teaspoon black peppercorns

½ teaspoon fennel seeds

2 bay leaves

Use a peeler to thinly slice the carrots into long, thin ribbons (about 2 lightly packed cups). Place the carrot ribbons in a heatproof medium bowl.

In a small saucepan set on medium heat, stir together the grape juice, vinegar, sugar, 1¾ teaspoons salt, the black peppercorns, fennel seeds, and bay leaves. Cook, stirring occasionally, until the sugar and salt are dissolved and the liquid starts to steam, 3 to 4 minutes. (You want the pickling liquid to be warm but not so hot that it cooks the carrots.) Pour the pickling liquid over the carrot ribbons and let cool completely, about 1 hour. Remove the bay leaves. Transfer to a container and store in the refrigerator until ready to use.

"This burger has a positive energy that makes me feel like I'm not only surviving, but thriving!" -EMILY

Stuffing

FROM THE KITCHEN OF: **PAM**

YIELD: **MAKES 8 TO 10 SERVINGS**

Most folks only think about stuffing during the holidays, and even then they just go to JojaMart and get the cheap mix. But in my family, stuffing was serious business—we'd have it year-round and fuss over all the little details. That meant sending the kids out to find wild hazelnuts and herbs (while the adults sat back with ice-cold beers . . .), a tradition I've kept alive with my Penny!

My family recipe also uses apples and cranberries to give the stuffing a seasonal tanginess. However, don't forget that the most important part of stuffing is the bread, so if you don't start off with a quality loaf, you'll be going nowhere fast! I'm not usually one to turn my nose up at boxed foods, but when it comes to stuffing, you have to go all out. So, don't skimp on any of the ingredients. You can thank me later, kid.

INGREDIENTS

½ cup (1 stick) plus 2 tablespoons **UNSALTED BUTTER**, plus more for greasing

1½ pounds **RUSTIC COUNTRY** or **SOURDOUGH BREAD**

½ cup blanched **RAW HAZELNUTS**

3 large **CELERY STALKS**, coarsely chopped

2 small **YELLOW ONIONS**, coarsely chopped

KOSHER SALT and **FRESHLY GROUND BLACK PEPPER**

2 small firm, tart **APPLES**, such as Granny Smith, unpeeled, cored and cut into ½-inch pieces

2 teaspoons chopped **FRESH THYME LEAVES**

1 teaspoon chopped **FRESH ROSEMARY LEAVES**

10 large **FRESH SAGE LEAVES**, thinly sliced

½ cup **DRIED CRANBERRIES**

3 cups **VEGETABLE STOCK** (page 25)

2 **LARGE EGGS**

Preheat the oven to 300°F. Generously grease a 9 by 13-inch baking dish.

Use a serrated knife to cut off the crust from the bread, then use your hands to tear the bread into large bite-size pieces (about 1 inch; 2.5 cm). Spread the bread pieces on a baking sheet and bake until the bread is slightly dried out, crispy in spots (but not browned), about 30 minutes, stirring the bread every 10 minutes. Let cool. Increase the oven temperature to 375°F.

Scatter the hazelnuts on a small baking sheet and toast in the oven until lightly browned and fragrant, 7 to 9 minutes, stirring several times to ensure the nuts toast evenly. Transfer to a cutting board, let cool completely, then coarsely chop the nuts.

In a large high-sided skillet set on medium heat, melt ½ cup (1 stick) of the butter. When butter is bubbling, add the celery and onions. Season with salt and pepper, and cook, stirring occasionally, until the vegetables are starting to soften, about 10 minutes. Add the apples, thyme, and rosemary, then season with salt and pepper. Cook until the vegetables and the apples are tender, about 15 minutes. Add the sage and dried cranberries, and cook, stirring constantly, for 1 minute. Taste the mixture and season with additional salt and pepper, if needed. (The mixture should be highly seasoned since it will help flavor the bread for the stuffing.) Spoon the mixture into an extra-large bowl, add the bread pieces and the hazelnuts, and stir to combine.

In a medium bowl, whisk together the stock and eggs until smooth. Pour the egg mixture over the stuffing mixture and stir until everything is evenly coated and most of the liquid has been absorbed into the bread (a little bit of liquid pooled at the bottom of the bowl is fine). Transfer the stuffing to the baking dish and let rest for 15 minutes.

Preheat the oven to 375°F.

Cut the remaining 2 tablespoons butter into small cubes. Dot the top of the stuffing with the butter and grind some black pepper over everything. Cover the dish with foil, and bake for 30 minutes. Uncover and continue to bake until the top is crispy and golden brown, about 30 additional minutes, rotating the baking dish once after 15 minutes.

Let the stuffing rest for 10 minutes, then serve.

"It's sure nice to be eating home-cooked meals again after four years of military rations."
-KENT

Super Meal

WARM GRAIN BOWL WITH FALL VEGGIES AND A GREEN DRESSING

| FROM THE KITCHEN OF: | KENT | YIELD: | MAKES 4 SERVINGS |

One of the upsides to having been stationed overseas is that I got to sample all sorts of cuisine from other cultures. This was before the war broke out, of course. There was this one dish I had pretty often; it was a nice mix of veggies and grains with a tangy green dressing, but what really stood out for me were the pomegranate seeds—it took only a couple of spoonfuls to perfect the dish. The little seeds burst as you bit into them, and they were sweet and sour at the same time. For some reason, it really appealed to me.

When I came home, I started trying to replicate that dish, and I think I finally cracked it. Cooked farro has this great texture that goes well with bok choy and roasted artichokes, and the herbs really bring out all those hidden flavors. You can make the dressing with or without anchovies; I've tried it both ways and they're both great. I usually end up making way more dressing than this recipe calls for, and then I just pour it on everything. It's that good!

INGREDIENTS

Farro
KOSHER SALT

2 cups **PEARLED FARRO,** rinsed

2 tablespoons **EXTRA-VIRGIN OLIVE OIL**

½ cup **DRIED CRANBERRIES**

FRESHLY GROUND BLACK PEPPER

Oven-Roasted Baby Artichokes and Bok Choy
2 large **LEMONS**

2 pounds (900 g) **BABY ARTICHOKES** (12 to 16, depending on size; see Queen's Tip)

2 tablespoons **VEGETABLE STOCK** (page 25) or **WATER**

2 tablespoons **EXTRA-VIRGIN OLIVE OIL**

2 **GARLIC CLOVES,** finely grated

¼ teaspoon **RED PEPPER FLAKES**

KOSHER SALT

6 **BABY BOK CHOY** (about 1 lb), halved lengthwise

1 tablespoon **WATER**

Avocado–Green Goddess Dressing

1 large ripe **AVOCADO**

¼ cup **FRESH LEMON JUICE** (from 1 large lemon)

¼ cup **EXTRA-VIRGIN OLIVE OIL**

¼ cup **WATER**, plus more as needed

2 **GARLIC CLOVES**, finely grated

¼ cup lightly packed **FRESH BASIL LEAVES**

¼ cup lightly packed **FRESH FLAT-LEAF PARSLEY LEAVES**

⅓ cup thinly sliced **SCALLIONS** (white and green parts)

1 tablespoon lightly packed **TARRAGON LEAVES**

2 **ANCHOVIES** packed in olive oil, drained and patted dry (optional)

KOSHER SALT and **FRESHLY GROUND BLACK PEPPER**

Assembly

¼ cup coarsely chopped **FRESH FLAT-LEAF PARSLEY**

½ cup **FRESH POMEGRANATE SEEDS** (arils)

FOR THE FARRO: Bring a large saucepan of lightly salted water to a boil over medium-high heat. Add the farro and cook until tender all the way through but retaining a nice chew, about 20 minutes.

Drain the farro well in a large fine-mesh strainer, then return to the saucepan. Stir in the olive oil and cranberries, and season with salt and pepper. Cover and let rest.

FOR THE ARTICHOKES AND BOK CHOY: Preheat the oven to 425°F.

Cut the lemons in half and squeeze the juice into a large bowl, setting aside 2 tablespoons of juice. Put 3 of the lemon halves in the bowl with the remaining juice. Set aside the remaining lemon half.

Fill the bowl with the lemon juice halfway with cold water. Working with 1 baby artichoke at a time, trim the stem to 1 inch, then use a peeler (preferably a Y-peeler) to peel off the tough dark green outer layer. Use your hands to snap off the tough, outer green leaves from around the artichoke until you reach the inner tender yellow leaves. Rub the yellow leaves and stem with the reserved lemon half.

Queen's Tip

If fresh baby artichokes are not available, substitute 12 ounces of thawed frozen quartered artichoke hearts.

Use a paring knife to trim away any tough green parts near the base of the artichoke, rubbing it with lemon as you work. Cut the top ¼ inch (6 mm) off the tender yellow leaves, then cut the artichoke in half from top to bottom. Use a small spoon to scrape out any fuzzy thistle that might be in the center. Add the 2 artichoke halves to the bowl of lemon water and repeat with the remaining artichokes.

In a 9 by 13-inch baking dish, combine the remaining 2 tablespoons lemon juice, the stock, olive oil, garlic, red pepper flakes, and a large pinch of salt. Drain the trimmed artichokes, then add to the dish and stir to coat well. Roast until the artichokes are fork-tender, 15 to 20 minutes, stirring once after 10 minutes. Keep the oven turned on.

RECIPE CONTINUES

Scatter the baby bok choy over the artichokes in the dish, sprinkle with the water, and season with additional salt. Use tongs to mix the bok choy with the artichokes and sauce, then return the baking dish to the oven and roast until the bok choy are crisp-tender and lightly browned in spots, 7 to 10 additional minutes.

FOR THE DRESSING: Cut the avocado in half, remove the pit, and scoop the flesh into a blender. Add the lemon juice, olive oil, ¼ cup water, the garlic, basil, parsley, scallions, tarragon, anchovies (if using), a pinch of salt, and several large grinds of black pepper. Cover with the lid and blend until smooth. The dressing should be thick and creamy, but you can thin it with a little additional water, if desired.

ASSEMBLE THE MEAL: Divide the farro among 4 shallow bowls. Sprinkle with the parsley, then top with the roasted artichokes and baby bok choy. Add the pomegranate seeds. Serve immediately, with the dressing on the side.

"Pomegranates are rich in antioxidants. . . . If only I could prescribe this dish to all my patients!" –HARVEY

Salmon Dinner

WITH AMARANTH PILAF AND KALE SALAD

YIELD: **MAKES 4 SERVINGS**

This one's always popular at the Stardrop Saloon when I make it the daily special, but I don't feel too bad about giving up my recipe. After all, folks stop in for the atmosphere and to socialize. And I'm sure plenty of them will keep on ordering that Salmon Dinner, even if they know how to make it at home. It might be a little complex for novice home cooks, but I have faith in your culinary skills.

It's important to keep an eye on the salmon and to keep spooning the citrus vinaigrette over it as it cooks. This helps it stay moist and flavorful; it's easy to overcook salmon, and no one wants a plate of dry fish! Serve it with a slice of pie or the dessert of your choice, and you've got yourself a full-course meal.

INGREDIENTS

Kale Salad

12 ounces **TUSCAN KALE** (about 2 large bunches), stems removed and leaves chopped into bite-size pieces

3 tablespoons **EXTRA-VIRGIN OLIVE OIL**

2 tablespoons **FRESH LEMON JUICE**

½ teaspoon **HONEY**

⅛ to ¼ teaspoon **RED PEPPER FLAKES**

KOSHER SALT

2 to 3 tablespoons **NUTRITIONAL YEAST**

1 cup **SEEDLESS RED GRAPES**, halved

Slow-Roasted Salmon with Citrus and Olive Oil

¼ cup **EXTRA-VIRGIN OLIVE OIL**

¼ cup **FRESH MANDARIN JUICE**, plus 1 small mandarin, peeled and sliced into 8 thin rounds

2 tablespoons **FRESH LEMON JUICE**, plus **1 SMALL LEMON**, sliced into 8 thin rounds

2 **GARLIC CLOVES**, finely grated

2 tablespoons **CAPERS** in brine, drained

KOSHER SALT and **FRESHLY GROUND BLACK PEPPER**

4 (6-oz) **SALMON FILLETS**, preferably center-cut, skin removed

Hand-torn **FRESH DILL**, for garnish	½ small **YELLOW ONION**, finely chopped	1½ cups **VEGETABLE STOCK** (page 25) or water
Amaranth Pilaf 2 tablespoons **UNSALTED BUTTER**	**KOSHER SALT** and **FRESHLY GROUND BLACK PEPPER**	1 cup **AMARANTH**
	2 **GARLIC CLOVES**, minced	½ teaspoon finely chopped **FRESH ROSEMARY LEAVES**

FOR THE KALE SALAD: Put the kale in a large bowl, drizzle with the olive oil, lemon juice, and honey, then season with the red pepper flakes and a pinch of salt. Use your hands to massage the kale until it wilts and becomes somewhat tender, about 2 minutes.

FOR THE SALMON: Preheat the oven to 300°F.

In a 9 by 13-inch baking dish, combine the olive oil, mandarin juice, lemon juice, garlic, capers, a large pinch of salt, and several large grinds of black pepper. Use a fork to whisk the vinaigrette together, smashing down on the capers to release their briny juices.

Season the salmon liberally on all sides with salt and pepper, then place the fish top side up in the baking dish. Spoon some of the vinaigrette over the salmon. Shingle the citrus slices over the top of the salmon, then spoon some of the vinaigrette over the lemon slices.

Bake until the fish is opaque, buttery, and starting to flake apart, 20 to 25 minutes, opening the oven and spooning the vinaigrette over the salmon several times. The timing for this will vary, depending on the thickness of your fish. Let the salmon rest for 5 minutes.

MEANWHILE, MAKE THE AMARANTH PILAF: In a medium saucepan over medium heat, melt the butter. Add the onion, season with salt and pepper, and cook, stirring occasionally, until softened, 5 to 7 minutes. Add the garlic and cook, stirring frequently, until softened,

about 2 minutes. Add the stock, increase the heat slightly, and bring to a boil, 3 to 4 minutes. Stir in the amaranth and rosemary, lower the heat to low, cover the saucepan with a lid, and cook until the amaranth has absorbed all the liquid, about 25 minutes. Let sit, covered, for 5 minutes. Fluff the amaranth with a fork and season with salt and pepper, if needed.

To serve, stir the nutritional yeast and halved red grapes into the kale salad. Divide the salad and the amaranth pilaf among 4 large serving plates. Place one salmon fillet on each plate and drizzle with some of the vinaigrette left in the baking dish. Sprinkle the dill on the fish and serve.

"Best thing on the menu by far; it's got all that lean protein from the salmon, and complex carbs to keep me energized through my workout. I'm getting sweaty just thinking about it." -ALEX

Salmon
Dinner
130

Blackberry
Cobbler
134

Blackberry Cobbler

FROM THE KITCHEN OF: **THE QUEEN OF SAUCE**

YIELD: **MAKES 6 TO 8 SERVINGS**

Ah, blackberries . . . those precious little nuggets of wild forest flavor! I don't think blackberries get the love they deserve. You're often lucky if you find one good recipe in a whole dessert cookbook! One of these days I think I might just make another cookbook with nothing but blackberry recipes. I'll be the Queen of Blackberry Sauce!

For now, though, I'll be content with one really smashing blackberry cobbler recipe. We'll go all in on blackberry flavor by using fresh fruit and preserves together in the filling, and then top it with spoonful after spoonful of old-fashioned buttermilk biscuit dough. And I don't think it'll come as a shock to anyone when I say that this cobbler pairs magnificently with a scoop of vanilla ice cream. You've got to let the cobbler rest and cool a little before digging in, though; I don't want to see any of you out there burning your tongues because you were too eager!

INGREDIENTS

1 tablespoon **MELTED UNSALTED BUTTER,** for greasing and brushing

1¼ cups (175 g) **ALL-PURPOSE FLOUR**

½ cup (100 g) **GRANULATED SUGAR**

1½ teaspoons **BAKING POWDER**

¼ teaspoon **GROUND CINNAMON**

KOSHER SALT

½ cup (1 stick; 110 g) **FROZEN UNSALTED BUTTER**

½ cup (120 ml) cold **BUTTERMILK**

¾ teaspoon **VANILLA EXTRACT**

¼ cup (75 g) **BLACKBERRY PRESERVES**

1½ pounds (680 g) **BLACKBERRIES** (5 to 6 cups)

3 tablespoons **CORNSTARCH**

1 tablespoon **RAW** or **TURBINADO SUGAR**

VANILLA ICE CREAM and/or **WHIPPED CREAM,** for serving

Preheat the oven to 375°F (190°C). Grease a 2-quart (1.9 L) baking dish with some of the melted butter.

In a medium bowl, combine the flour, 2 tablespoons (25 g) of the granulated sugar, the baking powder, cinnamon, and ½ teaspoon salt. Whisk to combine.

Grate the frozen butter on the large holes of a box grater, then add to the flour mixture and use your fingers to work the butter into the flour until it resembles coarse crumbs. In a small bowl, stir together the buttermilk and vanilla, then drizzle over the flour mixture and use a rubber spatula to mix until a fairly rough dough just starts to form. Switch to your hands and gently mix until it just comes together into a soft dough (do not overmix). Chill in the refrigerator while you put together the filling.

In a medium bowl, whisk the blackberry preserves until smooth, then add the blackberries, remaining 6 tablespoons (75 g) sugar, and ¼ teaspoon salt. Stir gently to combine. Sprinkle the cornstarch over the berries and stir gently again until well combined.

Spoon the blackberry mixture into the baking dish. Drop 9 rounded spoonfuls of the biscuit dough on top of the berries. Brush the biscuits with any remaining melted butter, and sprinkle the tops with the raw or turbinado sugar.

Place the cobbler on a baking sheet and bake until the fruit filling is vigorously bubbling (in the center and on the edges) and the biscuits are deep golden brown, puffed, and cooked through, about 50 minutes, rotating the baking sheet once after 25 minutes. Rest the cobbler for 30 minutes before serving it warm, topped with vanilla ice cream and/or whipped cream.

 "I love the crunchy, sugary crust on top, and that dark purple color is really appealing to me. Don't tell anyone, but I totally did burn my tongue on some cobbler once when I was little. . . . Oh, who am I kidding? It just happened last year!" –ABIGAIL

Pumpkin Pie

FROM THE KITCHEN OF:	THE QUEEN OF SAUCE	YIELD: MAKES 8 TO 10 SERVINGS

No fall feast would be complete without Pumpkin Pie. And no pumpkin pie would be complete without an exotic blend of warming spices. Of course, there's also the added bonus of having your home blessed by their magnificent bouquet while the little treasure bakes! Indeed, there are few things I love more than the cozy feel of a kitchen with a pumpkin pie in the oven.

Our pumpkin pie will use fresh, roasted pumpkins for a depth of flavor the likes of which you've never experienced before. All the classic spices bring their magic to the mix to give our pie that iconic pumpkin pie flavor. It's everything you love about pumpkin pie turned up to 11, with brown sugar and nuts blended right into the crust for a taste and texture that puts other pies to shame!

INGREDIENTS

Pumpkin Pie

1 small **SUGAR PUMPKIN** (about 2¾ lb; 1.3 kg)

½ cup (1 stick; 110 g) cold **UNSALTED BUTTER**, cut into small cubes

1½ cups (210 g) **ALL-PURPOSE FLOUR**, plus additional for dusting

¼ cup (30 g) blanched **RAW HAZELNUTS**

¼ cup (25 g) **RAW PECANS**

1 cup (200 g) plus 2 tablespoons packed **LIGHT BROWN SUGAR**

KOSHER SALT

⅓ cup (80 ml) **ICE WATER**

1½ teaspoons **APPLE CIDER VINEGAR**

2 **LARGE EGGS** plus 1 **EGG YOLK**, at room temperature

⅔ cup (160 ml) **HEAVY CREAM**, at room temperature

⅓ cup (80 ml) **WHOLE MILK**, at room temperature

1½ teaspoons **GROUND CINNAMON**

½ teaspoon **GROUND GINGER**

¼ teaspoon freshly grated **NUTMEG**

⅛ teaspoon **GROUND ALLSPICE**

4 teaspoons **CORNSTARCH**

Serving

1 cup (240 ml) chilled **HEAVY CREAM**

3 tablespoons **PURE MAPLE SYRUP**

KOSHER SALT

Toasted **HAZELNUTS** and/or toasted **PECANS**

FOR THE PIE: Preheat the oven to 400°F (200°C). Line a baking sheet with parchment paper.

Carefully cut the pumpkin in half. Use a spoon to remove the seeds (save to roast and eat as a snack) and scrape out as many of the strings as possible. Use your hands to liberally rub water all over the inside and outside of the halves, then place cut side down on the baking sheet. Roast until the pumpkin is very tender (a fork should go through the skin and flesh without any effort), 45 to 55 minutes, rotating once after 25 minutes. Let cool completely.

Put the butter cubes in the freezer for 20 minutes.

In the bowl of a food processor, combine the 1½ cups (210 g) flour, the raw hazelnuts, raw pecans, 2 tablespoons brown sugar, and ¾ teaspoon salt and pulse several times until the nuts are finely ground. Add the cold butter and pulse until the mixture resembles coarse breadcrumbs. Stir the ice water and vinegar in a small bowl, then drizzle ¼ cup (60 ml) over the mixture. Pulse several times, until the mixture

forms a rough dough that holds together when you squeeze it in your hand, adding more water, 1 teaspoon at a time, if needed.

Turn out the dough onto a large piece of plastic wrap, press into a mostly smooth cube, and flatten into a 1-inch (2.5 cm) disk. Wrap tightly and chill in the refrigerator until firm (but not hard), about 45 minutes.

On a lightly floured surface, roll out the dough into a 13-inch (33 cm) round that is a little bit thinner than ⅛ inch (3 mm) thick. Carefully roll the dough around the rolling pin, then unroll into a 9½-inch (24 cm) deep-dish pie plate. The dough is tender, so it might crack while being moved to the pie plate. That is absolutely okay; just use your fingers to gently push the cracked pieces back together. Gently press the dough down into the pie plate and trim the edges, leaving a 1-inch (2.5 cm) overhang. Use any dough scraps to fill holes or cracks in the dough. Fold the overhanging dough under itself and crimp the edges with your fingers. Pierce the bottom all over with a fork. Refrigerate the crust until it is firm, about 30 minutes.

RECIPE CONTINUES

Put a baking sheet on the lowest rack of the oven and preheat the oven to 375°F (190°C).

Line the chilled crust with a double layer of parchment paper that extends over the edges of the crust. Fill the parchment paper to the very brim of the crust with dry rice or dried beans. Roughly fold the overhanging paper loosely over the edges of the pie crust.

Bake the crust on the baking sheet until the edges of the dough start to feel dry and are set, 20 to 25 minutes. Carefully remove the foil and the rice or beans. Return the crust to the oven and continue to bake until the edges of the crust are lightly browned and the bottom and sides are just cooked through (they might be pale at this point, but that is okay), 10 to 15 additional minutes. Let the crust cool slightly on a wire rack while you make the filling. Leave the baking sheet in the oven and leave the oven turned on.

Scoop the flesh of the pumpkin into a food processor and blend until very smooth. Measure out 1¾ cups (400 g) of the puree and place in a large bowl. (Reserve any remaining puree for another use.) Add the eggs and egg yolk, ⅔ cup (160 ml) of the room-temperature

cream, the milk, the remaining 1 cup (200 g) of brown sugar, the cinnamon, ginger, nutmeg, allspice, and ½ teaspoon salt. Whisk until smooth. Add the cornstarch and whisk again very vigorously until smooth again. Pour into the warm crust.

Place the pie on the hot baking sheet and bake until the edges of the filling are set but the center is still fairly jiggly (it might seem too loose, but it will set up fully once cooled), about 50 minutes, rotating the baking sheet once after 30 minutes. If the edges of the crust start to get too brown before the filling is finished cooking, cover them with aluminum foil or a pie crust shield. Remove from the oven and cool completely on the hot baking sheet, 4 to 5 hours.

TOP AND SERVE THE PIE: Combine the chilled cream, the maple syrup, and a pinch of salt in a medium bowl. Use a large whisk or electric hand mixer to whip the cream to medium peaks. Garnish the cooled pie with the toasted hazelnuts and/or pecans. Slice into 8 to 10 wedges and serve topped with dollops of the maple whipped cream.

"I've always loved this season; all the beautiful colors, the chill in the air . . . or maybe it's just because my birthday is coming up! This year, all I ask for is a pumpkin pie . . . and a pumpkin for each of my cows!"
-MARNIE

Cranberry Candy

A CRANBERRY SYRUP FOR SODAS AND MIXED DRINKS

FROM THE KITCHEN OF:	THE QUEEN OF SAUCE	YIELD: MAKES 4 SERVINGS

If _sour_ is the first word that comes to mind when you think of cranberries, try this on for size. We're going to make a sweet cranberry syrup that'll make you say, "Wow, zinga!!" When I say sweet, I mean SWEET. I don't call it candy for nothing! Mix it with some apple cider and we've got ourselves a cranberry concoction that is second to none. You can also add the syrup to sparkling water for a less intensely sweet treat.

And for those adult get-togethers, you can easily make a more mature version by simply using hard cider. Just be sure to drink in moderation; the sweetness can mask the taste of the alcohol and make it easy to drink quickly. Pace yourself!

INGREDIENTS

1½ cups **FRESH CRANBERRIES** or thawed **FROZEN CRANBERRIES**

1 cup packed **LIGHT BROWN SUGAR**

1¼ cups **WATER**

KOSHER SALT

¾ teaspoon **VANILLA EXTRACT**

ICE CUBES, as needed

3 cups **SPARKLING APPLE-CRANBERRY CIDER** or **PLAIN APPLE CIDER** (see Queen's Tip)

FRESH CRANBERRIES or thawed **FROZEN CRANBERRIES**, for garnish

In a small saucepan over medium-low heat, stir together the cranberries, brown sugar, water, and a pinch of salt. Cook, stirring occasionally, until the mixture starts to simmer, then continue to simmer until the cranberries have all burst and become very tender, 15 to 25 minutes. Turn off the heat and stir in the vanilla.

Strain the mixture through a sieve into a medium bowl, pressing down on the cranberries to extract as much liquid as possible. Make sure to scrape off the jammy pulp that comes through the strainer and stir it into the syrup. (You should have only the cranberry skins and seeds in the strainer.) If you have less than 1½ cups of syrup after straining, add enough water to reach that amount. Stir the syrup until smooth, then let cool.

Divide the syrup among 4 tall glasses. Transfer the remaining syrup to a glass jar with a lid, where it can be stored in the refrigerator for up to 14 days. Fill the glasses with ice cubes, then top with the sparkling cider. Use a long spoon to give each drink a good stir, and garnish with several cranberries, then serve immediately.

"Mom only lets me have one glass on special occasions. She says she doesn't want me bouncing off the walls all night. It's not fair! Sam gets to have two, and he doesn't bounce off the walls." -VINCENT

WINTER

Dishes that warm the body, heart, and soul

Winter's cold makes it feel like the world is going to sleep; snowflakes slowly pile up, covering the land in a blanket of white once again. Personally, I enjoy going for a walk on freshly fallen snow, hearing it crunch beneath my feet with each step in the otherwise silent snowscape. It may be cold out there, but it's worth getting outside in the sunlight to keep your spirits high!

It's also important to keep warm and well fed, and I've got plenty of recipes to help out on that front. While less green produce is available, there are many storage crops that can keep you cooking all winter long, such as root vegetables, cabbages, mushrooms, and pumpkins. If you're in the mood for some hearty, stick-to-your-ribs fare, you can't go wrong with Fried Mushrooms. If you're looking for some intense flavor and heat, give Pepper Poppers a try; they'll get your legs moving at top speed! Or, if you'd like something a little more cozy, might I suggest Eggplant Parmesan or homemade Spaghetti with a mushroom Bolognese sauce? And if you're ready for something unique, why not take a crack at Seafoam Pudding?

Whether you're snowed in for the season or have escaped to more forgiving climates, you're bound to find plenty here to keep you warm and satisfied. I might not be able to help with the lack of sunlight, but I'll do everything in my power to help keep your stomach full and your spirits high!

Roots Platter

FROM THE KITCHEN OF: **THE QUEEN OF SAUCE**

YIELD: **MAKES 2 TO 4**

Ah, roots! The fruits of winter! These hearty little guys are packed with nutrients and starches to keep you energized and warm, no matter how cold it gets. And when you roast them with some olive oil, magical things begin to happen; their flavors evolve as they soften, creating a complex dance of sweet and savory that will keep you coming back for more. These earthy morsels are begging for a bright, zesty counterpoint, so we'll be introducing them to a kale and walnut pesto; it's a match made in heaven!

INGREDIENTS

3 cups lightly packed coarsely chopped **CURLY KALE LEAVES**

½ cup plus 3 tablespoons **EXTRA-VIRGIN OLIVE OIL**, plus more as needed

KOSHER SALT and **FRESHLY GROUND BLACK PEPPER**

⅓ cup coarsely chopped **RAW WALNUTS**

1 **GARLIC CLOVE**

¼ cup packed **FRESH FLAT-LEAF PARSLEY LEAVES**

3 tablespoons grated **PARMESAN CHEESE**, plus shavings for garnish

8 ounces trimmed whole **BABY PURPLE AND ORANGE CARROTS** (6 to 8 total), scrubbed

8 ounces trimmed small **TOKYO TURNIPS** (about 6), scrubbed and quartered

8 ounces **CELERY ROOT**, peeled and cut into ¾-inch cubes (about 2 cups)

8 ounces **RUTABAGA**, peeled and cut into ¾-inch cubes (about 2 cups)

1 **SMALL LEMON**, cut in half

Preheat the oven to 375° F.

Put the curly kale leaves in a medium bowl. Drizzle with 2 tablespoons of the olive oil and season lightly with salt and pepper. Use your hands to massage the kale until it just starts to wilt, about 1 minute.

Scatter the walnuts on a small baking sheet and toast in the oven until lightly browned and fragrant, 6 to 8 minutes, stirring several times to ensure the nuts toast evenly. Transfer to a small bowl and let cool. Keep the oven turned on.

Put the garlic in a food processor and pulse several times to finely chop. Add the walnuts, massaged kale, and the parsley. Season with salt and pepper, and pulse several times until coarsely chopped. Add the grated Parmesan and pulse several times until just combined. With the processor running, slowly stream in 6 tablespoons of the olive oil and blend until smooth. Transfer to a small bowl and press plastic wrap directly on top of the pesto.

Place a large baking sheet on the bottom rack of the oven and increase the oven heat to 450°F.

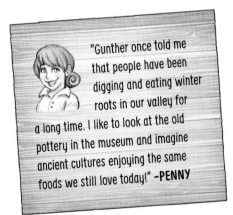

"Gunther once told me that people have been digging and eating winter roots in our valley for a long time. I like to look at the old pottery in the museum and imagine ancient cultures enjoying the same foods we still love today!" –PENNY

Queen's Tip

Transfer any leftover kale pesto to an airtight container and store in the refrigerator for up to 5 days or in the freezer for up to 1 month.

In a large bowl, toss the carrots, turnips, celery root, and rutabaga with the remaining 3 tablespoons olive oil until well coated. Season liberally with salt and pepper, and toss once more. Scatter the vegetables in a single layer on the hot baking sheet and roast until tender and deeply browned in spots, 25 to 30 minutes, stirring the vegetables once after 15 minutes. Depending on the size of the carrots, they might roast more quickly than the other vegetables. Check them at the 15-minute mark and remove if they are already tender, then let the remaining vegetables continue to roast until also tender.

Give the kale pesto a good stir and season with additional salt and pepper, if needed. The pesto might thicken slightly as it sits; stir in a touch more olive oil if you would prefer it thinner. Spread a couple large spoonfuls of the pesto onto the bottom of a large serving platter and squeeze the juice from half the lemon on top (see Queen's Tip). Scatter the roasted vegetables on top of the pesto, then squeeze the remaining lemon half over the hot vegetables. Nestle dollops of the remaining kale pesto into the vegetables, garnish with the shaved Parmesan cheese, and serve.

Strange Bun and Void Mayonnaise

LOBSTER IN A SOFT BUN WITH A GARLIC MAYONNAISE DIP

FROM THE KITCHEN OF: **SHANE**

YIELD: **MAKES 6 BUNS**

The other day I was in Zuzu City for a Tunnelers game, and I decided to check out this weird curiosity shop across the street on my way home. I was just about to leave when something caught my eye: a jet-black magazine half-hidden behind a bookcase. It was all covered in cobwebs and smelled awful, but the weirdest thing was that every page inside had the same handwritten recipe on it . . . something called "Strange Bun."

I only know how to cook microwaved food, but I thought you might want to try it out.

INGREDIENTS

½ cup (120 ml) **WHOLE MILK**

1⅔ cups (230 g) plus 3 tablespoons **BREAD FLOUR**

3 tablespoons **UNSALTED BUTTER**, at room temperature, plus more for greasing

3 tablespoons **MALTED MILK POWDER**

2 tablespoons packed **DARK BROWN SUGAR**

KOSHER SALT

1 (¼-oz; 7 g) packet **INSTANT YEAST**

½ cup (120 ml) **BUTTERMILK**, at room temperature

2 **LARGE EGGS**, at room temperature

1 cup (140 g) **ALL-PURPOSE FLOUR**

2 whole **LOBSTERS** (about 1½ lb; 680 g each)

½ cup (l stick; 110 g) **SALTED BUTTER**

FRESHLY GROUND BLACK PEPPER

6 large **SAGE LEAVES**, thinly sliced

2 teaspoons finely grated **LEMON ZEST**

2 **GARLIC CLOVES**, finely grated

VOID MAYONNAISE, for serving (recipe follows)

Special Equipment
6-cup **JUMBO MUFFIN TIN** and 6 (6-inch; 15 cm) **WOODEN SKEWERS**

In a medium saucepan, whisk together the whole milk and 3 tablespoons of the bread flour until smooth. Place the saucepan over low heat and cook the mixture, whisking constantly, until thick and like cake batter, 7 to 9 minutes. Transfer the milk mixture to a small bowl and let cool until just barely warm to the touch, 5 to 10 minutes.

Lightly grease a large bowl with a little butter.

In another large bowl, whisk together the malted milk powder, brown sugar, 2 teaspoons salt, the yeast, buttermilk, and 1 egg until well combined. Add the remaining 1⅔ cups (230 g) bread flour, the all-purpose flour, and the milk mixture. Use a rubber spatula to stir the ingredients together until mostly combined and resembling a very shaggy dough. (There will still be a good amount of flour at the bottom of the bowl, and that is okay as long as the mixture is no longer wet.) Using your hands, continue to mix until you have a fairly smooth dough. Add the 3 tablespoons butter, 1 tablespoon at a time, using your hands to work the butter into the dough before adding more. Every time you add more butter, the dough will start to feel greasier, but that is okay. Use one hand to knead the dough while you use your other hand to hold down the bowl. Use the rubber spatula to scrape down the sticky side of the bowl as needed. Continue kneading the dough in the bowl until it is no longer wet and sticky, 3 to 5 minutes.

Turn out the dough onto a clean flat surface and continue kneading (now with both hands) until smooth and elastic, 5 to 7 minutes. Shape the dough into a ball, place it in the greased bowl, and turn to coat with the grease. Cover the bowl and let the dough rest at room temperature until puffed to almost double its size, about 2 hours.

Lightly grease the cups of a 6-cup large-cup muffin tin.

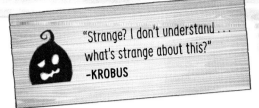

"Strange? I don't understand . . . what's strange about this?"
–KROBUS

Deflate the dough and gently press it into a rectangle (the size really doesn't matter). Divide the dough into 6 equal pieces. Use your hands to roll each piece into a 16-inch (40 cm) rope about ½ inch (1.3 cm) thick.

Starting at one end, roll each rope into a semi-conical spiral shape with a larger base and 2 coils that get slightly smaller as you work upward. The second coil will be almost the same size as the base, but the third coil on the top will be much smaller than the first two. Tuck the second end of the dough into the top of the bun and place the buns into the muffin cups as you form them. Nudge a 6-inch (15 cm) wooden skewer pointed side up into the very center of each bun.

Let the buns rest, uncovered, at room temperature until puffy and squishy like jumbo marshmallows, about 1 hour. The fully puffed buns should fill most of the muffin cups. After they puff up, the buns might end up leaning over. Use the wooden skewers to gently lift the buns and coax them so they sit straight again. Don't be concerned if they are not perfect; the imperfection will add to the "strangeness" of the buns.

About 40 minutes into the buns' second proof, preheat the oven to 350°F (175°C).

In a small bowl, whisk together the remaining egg and a splash of water. Brush the egg wash lightly onto the risen buns. Bake the buns until golden brown all over and the dough is cooked through, about 30 minutes, rotating the baking sheet once after 20 minutes. Transfer the buns from the muffin cups to a wire rack to cool completely.

RECIPE CONTINUES

Remove the wooden skewers and use a small paring knife to make a roughly 2-inch (5 cm) opening at the top of each bun, then use your fingers to carefully hollow out the buns, leaving a ½-inch (1.3 cm) wall on the sides and bottom. (Save the bun tops and any extra pieces to make fresh bread crumbs, if desired.) Loosely cover the buns.

Bring a large pot of salted water to a boil over medium-high heat. Fill an extra-large bowl with ice water and season it generously with salt.

Add the lobsters to the pot, cover with a lid, and boil until the shells are bright red and the meat is cooked through, 8 to 10 minutes. Transfer the lobsters directly to the ice bath to cool.

Pat the lobsters dry with a kitchen towel. Remove the meat from the claws, tails, and legs and roughly chop into bite-size chunks; you should have about 2½ cups (340 g). Chill the lobster meat.

In a medium saucepan over medium heat, melt the salted butter. Add several large grinds of black pepper and continue to cook, stirring frequently, until light brown specks start to form and the butter smells nutty, 7 to 10 minutes. Turn off the heat, add the sage, lemon zest, and grated garlic, and warm for 1 minute in the residual heat. (Be careful during this step because the mixture will get quite foamy and might sputter.) Add the lobster and stir to combine in the warm butter sauce. Season with additional salt and pepper, if needed.

Divide the lobster mixture among the 6 hollowed-out buns. Drizzle any extra butter sauce over the lobster and serve immediately, accompanied by the mayonnaise.

VOID MAYONNAISE

Makes 1 scant cup (190 g)

5 black garlic cloves

¼ teaspoon food-grade finely ground activated charcoal powder

1 tablespoon fresh lemon juice

1 large egg yolk, at room temperature

2 teaspoons Dijon mustard

Kosher salt

¾ cup (175 ml) neutral oil, such as light olive oil

Use the back of a large kitchen knife to smash the garlic until it forms a paste (about 2 teaspoons). Transfer to a small bowl.

In a medium bowl, combine the activated charcoal and 2 teaspoons of the lemon juice. Whisk until the charcoal is dissolved. Add the egg yolk, Dijon mustard, and a large pinch of salt, and whisk again until smooth.

Very slowly, begin to drizzle the oil into the bowl with the egg mixture, whisking constantly and vigorously. At the beginning, you want to add the oil nearly drop by drop to form an emulsion. Make sure any oil you add is incorporated into the egg mixture before adding more.

When you have added nearly half the oil, increase the speed at which you add the oil but still add it slowly and continue to whisk constantly and vigorously. At this point, your arm will be tired, but muster your strength and persevere (or ask a friend to help out).

When the mixture is thick and creamy, add the remaining 1 teaspoon lemon juice, a small splash of water, and the black garlic paste. Whisk until smooth. If the mayonnaise is super thick, whisk in additional water, a small splash at a time, until you reach your desired consistency. Season to taste with additional salt, if needed.

Fried Mushroom

WITH A MALT VINEGAR RANCH DRESSING

FROM THE KITCHEN OF: DEMETRIUS

YIELD: MAKES 4 TO 6 SERVINGS

Mushrooms are a nutritional powerhouse; I like to eat them for their neuro-regenerative properties with regard to the prefrontal cortex, as well as their optimal macronutrient composition. These fantastic fungi work well as a support in so many dishes, but I've got a simple recipe that makes them the star of the show. The mushrooms are coated in a beer batter and fried until they reach the perfect crunch.

The beer introduces tiny bubbles of carbon dioxide into the batter, along with other compounds that help stabilize those bubbles to create a soft, airy texture with an optimal crunch-to-moisture-ratio (CTMR). Once they're nicely fried, serve them up alongside your favorite dipping sauce; I recommend Robin's famous Malt Vinegar Ranch Dressing.

INGREDIENTS

NEUTRAL HIGH-HEAT COOKING OIL, for frying

1¼ cups **ALL-PURPOSE FLOUR**

¼ cup **CORNSTARCH**

KOSHER SALT and **FRESHLY GROUND BLACK PEPPER**

1 teaspoon **GRANULATED GARLIC**

½ teaspoon **ONION POWDER**

½ teaspoon **BAKING POWDER**

Pinch of **CAYENNE**

1 **LARGE EGG WHITE**, cold

¾ cup cold **BUTTERMILK**

¾ cup (6 fl oz) cold **LAGER** or **INDIA PALE ALE BEER**, plus more as needed

8 ounces fresh small **CREMINI MUSHROOMS**, halved if large

8 ounces fresh **WILD MUSHROOMS** (morels, chanterelles, hen of the woods, oyster mushrooms, etc.), torn or cut into large bite-size pieces

MALT VINEGAR RANCH DRESSING (recipe follows)

Fill a large Dutch oven with 1 inch of oil and heat to 350°F over medium-high heat.

In a large bowl, whisk together ¾ cup of the flour, the cornstarch, 2 teaspoons salt, several large grinds of black pepper, the granulated garlic, onion powder, baking powder, and cayenne.

In a medium bowl, combine the egg white, buttermilk, and beer. Whisk until smooth, then add to the flour mixture and whisk until just combined (a few lumps are fine). The consistency should be similar to thin crepe batter.

Set a wire rack on a large baking sheet. Place the remaining ½ cup flour in a medium bowl. In 3 batches, toss the mushrooms with the flour until well coated, shaking off the excess. Place the mushrooms in the batter and turn to coat. Using tongs or your fingers (be extra careful if doing this with your fingers), pick up the mushrooms one by one and add them to the hot oil. Fry, stirring with a spider or slotted spoon occasionally, until golden brown and crispy, 3 to 4 minutes. Transfer the fried mushrooms to the rack and sprinkle with additional salt. Allow the oil to come back up to temperature and fry the remaining mushrooms. If the batter starts to become thicker, whisk in a splash of cold beer to return it to the original consistency.

Arrange the fried mushrooms on a serving platter and serve immediately, with the dressing for dipping.

MALT VINEGAR RANCH DRESSING

Makes about 1¼ cups

⅓ cup mayonnaise

⅓ cup sour cream

⅓ cup buttermilk

2 tablespoons malt vinegar

¼ teaspoon granulated sugar

1 garlic clove, finely grated

3 tablespoons thinly sliced fresh chives

2 tablespoons finely chopped fresh flat-leaf parsley leaves

1 tablespoon finely chopped fresh dill

Kosher salt and freshly ground black pepper

In a medium bowl, combine the mayonnaise, sour cream, buttermilk, vinegar, sugar, garlic, chives, parsley, and dill. Season with salt and pepper, and whisk to combine. Serve immediately or transfer to an airtight container and store in the refrigerator for up to 7 days.

"Now, that's the stuff; this reminds me of my mining days, having a beer and some grub with the boys after a long shift. This vinegar ranch dip is a lot fancier than the cheap ketchup they served back then, and tastier, too." —GEORGE

Tom Kha Soup

| FROM THE KITCHEN OF: **SANDY** | YIELD: **MAKES 4 TO 6 SERVINGS** |

You know, it actually gets pretty cold here in the desert some nights. If I start to get a chill, I like to curl up with a good book and a nice hot bowl of soup. One of my go-to recipes is this delicious Tom Kha Soup; it's got a lovely blend of shrimp and coconut flavor that's warm and satisfying, and lots of mushrooms and greens to fill you up . . . along with chilies for some extra color and a spicy kick.

But, honey, don't throw out those shrimp shells! They make a great stock that's part of the secret to why this soup is so irresistible, along with the coconut milk. I've got coconuts aplenty out here, but it shouldn't be too tough to find coconut milk, no matter where you are. Serve up a bowl of this fantastic soup alongside some Mango Sticky Rice, and we're in paradise!

INGREDIENTS

2 **LEMONGRASS STALKS**

6 **MAKRUT LIME LEAVES**

1 (2-inch) piece **GALANGAL**, peeled and sliced into ¼-inch rounds

2 cups **SHRIMP STOCK** (page 113)

2 cups **WATER**

2 to 4 **THAI BIRD'S-EYE CHILIES**, halved, as desired

12 ounces **FRESH BROWN SHIMEJI MUSHROOMS**, left whole, or **CREMINI MUSHROOMS**, quartered

2¾ cups **UNSWEETENED COCONUT MILK**

⅓ cup **FISH SAUCE**, plus more as needed

1 tablespoon packed **PALM SUGAR** or **LIGHT BROWN SUGAR**

4 **GARLIC CLOVES**, thinly sliced

1 pound large or extra-large **SHRIMP**, peeled and deveined, tails removed (reserve shells for Shrimp Stock, page 113)

KOSHER SALT

⅓ cup **FRESH LIME JUICE** (from about 3 limes), plus more as needed

Fresh **CILANTRO LEAVES**, for topping

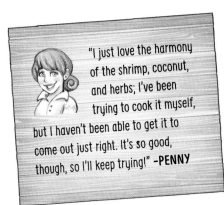

"I just love the harmony of the shrimp, coconut, and herbs; I've been trying to cook it myself, but I haven't been able to get it to come out just right. It's so good, though, so I'll keep trying!" -PENNY

In a medium saucepan over medium-high heat, combine the lemongrass, lime leaves, galangal, Shrimp Stock, and water and bring to a boil. Reduce the heat and simmer, partially covered with a lid, for 15 minutes. Remove the lid, stir in the chilies, re-cover, and continue to simmer for an additional 15 minutes.

Trim off the root ends of the shimeji mushrooms and use your hands to separate them into small pieces.

Stir the coconut milk, fish sauce, palm sugar, and garlic into the saucepan. Add the mushrooms, return the liquid to a simmer, and gently cook until the mushrooms and garlic are tender, 12 to 15 minutes.

Use a sharp knife to trim the lemongrass stalks so you are left with 3 inches on the bottom of each stalk. (Discard the tops or reserve to make Vegetable Stock, page 25.) Split the lemongrass bottoms in half lengthwise and use your hands to peel away the tough outermost layers. Turn each piece so that it is cut side down and use the back of the knife to gently hit each piece several times. (This will help the lemongrass to better flavor the soup.)

Lightly season the shrimp with salt and add it to the hot broth. Cook, stirring frequently, until the shrimp are just cooked through, 3 to 4 minutes, depending on size. Stir in the lime juice, then taste for seasoning; it should be a blend of sweet, salty, and sour. Adjust as needed with additional fish sauce or lime juice.

Ladle the soup into individual bowls, top with the cilantro leaves, and serve immediately (see Queen's Tip).

Queen's Tip

The lemongrass, lime leaves, chilies, and galangal are left in the soup to help flavor it and to keep the broth fragrant, but they are not meant to be eaten, so advise your guests accordingly.

Tom Kha
Soup
154

Pepper
Poppers
158

Pepper Poppers

FROM THE KITCHEN OF: **SHANE**

YIELD: **MAKES 20 POPPERS**

You know I'm not a food snob or anything, but I've got standards when it comes to the things I like. Sure, if I'm feeling lazy, I'll just grab a box of the premade pepper poppers from the freezer and throw them in the microwave. But they're kind of bland. Sometimes I'm in the mood for something spicier, and that's when I break out this recipe. The peppers are baked instead of fried, which is a lot easier. And if you have any left over, you can throw them on a frozen pizza the next day.

Sometimes Jas helps me make them, and I have her wear gloves to protect her hands from the jalapeños. If you handle them bare-handed with any cuts on your fingers, you'll be squawking like an egg-laying hen. Don't say I didn't warn you! And whatever you do, don't touch your eyes! I learned that one the hard way.

INGREDIENTS

5 large **GREEN JALAPEÑOS**, halved lengthwise, seeds and membranes removed (see Queen's Tip)

5 large **RED JALAPEÑOS**, halved lengthwise, seeds and membranes removed (see Queen's Tip)

1 tablespoon **EXTRA-VIRGIN OLIVE OIL**

KOSHER SALT

6 ounces **CREAM CHEESE**, at room temperature

2 tablespoons **MAYONNAISE**

4 ounces **PEPPER JACK CHEESE**, shredded

4 **PICKLED JALAPEÑO SLICES**, finely chopped

1 **SCALLION**, thinly sliced (white and green parts)

1 **GARLIC CLOVE**, finely grated

¼ teaspoon **SMOKED PAPRIKA**

1 cup **CORN FLAKES**

1 tablespoon **UNSALTED BUTTER**, melted

FRESHLY GROUND BLACK PEPPER

"If you handle the peppers and then touch your eyes, it can sting for hours. Just don't try to rinse out your eyes with beer." -SHANE

Preheat the oven to 425°F.

Place the jalapeños on a large baking sheet and brush all over with the olive oil, then season lightly with salt. Roast until the peppers are just starting to become tender, about 5 minutes. Let cool slightly. Keep the oven on and reduce the temperature to 375°F.

In a medium bowl, combine the cream cheese, mayonnaise, cheese, pickled jalapeños, scallion, garlic, and smoked paprika. Stir until well combined. Taste the filling and season with salt, if needed.

Use your fingers to coarsely crumble the corn flakes into a small bowl. Add the melted butter, a good pinch of salt, and a couple grinds of black pepper. Use your fingers to mix until the corn flakes are well coated.

Fill each jalapeño halfway with some of the cream cheese filling (about 1 tablespoon each). Use the back of a small spoon to flatten the filling and remove any excess that goes up higher than the edge of the jalapeños.

Do not overstuff, or the filling will ooze out. (Depending on the size of your jalapeños, you might have a little filling left over. Save it to spread on crackers or use as a spread for a spiced-up grilled cheese sandwich.) Sprinkle the tops of the filled jalapeños with the buttered corn flakes.

Place the filled jalapeños in the oven and bake until tender, the filling is hot and melty, and the corn flake topping is very crispy, about 15 minutes. Let cool for 5 minutes, then transfer to a platter and serve immediately.

Queen's Tip
For a less spicy version, use miniature sweet peppers in place of the jalapeños.

Eggplant Parmesan

WITH GUS'S FAMOUS MARINARA SAUCE

FROM THE KITCHEN OF: LEWIS

YIELD: MAKES 8 TO 12 SERVINGS

Whenever the governor comes over for dinner, he always requests my homemade Eggplant Parmesan. Can't say I blame him. Eggplant has always been a favorite of mine, ever since I first tasted one from your grandfather's farm . . . oh . . . must have been more than forty years ago. Just bread some slices of eggplant, layer them with mozzarella and Gus's Famous Marinara Sauce, and bake until bubbling. Your guests will be champing at the bit when they catch the first whiff of that fragrant aroma. And as a bonus, this dish has got plenty of fiber. You can thank me next year at the ballot box!

Eggplant is really good at taking on the flavors of foods it's cooked with, especially if you prepare it properly. The flesh can be a little bitter on its own, but a little salt takes care of that. The salt pulls water out of the eggplant, and the bitter flavor comes out with it. Harvey says the process is called "osmosis." It all sounds like wizardry if you ask me, but it's hard to argue with the results!

INGREDIENTS

2 pounds medium **EGGPLANT** (about 2 total), sliced into ½-inch rounds

KOSHER SALT

2½ cups **PANKO**

¾ cup grated **PARMESAN CHEESE**

1½ teaspoons **DRIED OREGANO**

1½ teaspoons **GRANULATED GARLIC**

FRESHLY GROUND BLACK PEPPER

1 cup **ALL-PURPOSE FLOUR**

3 **LARGE EGGS**

NEUTRAL HIGH-HEAT COOKING OIL, for frying

4 cups **GUS'S FAMOUS MARINARA SAUCE** (recipe follows)

1 (15-oz) container **WHOLE-MILK RICOTTA**, drained

4 ounces **GOAT CHEESE (CHÈVRE)**, at room temperature

2 tablespoons **HEAVY CREAM**

2 tablespoons chopped **FRESH FLAT-LEAF PARSLEY LEAVES**

12 ounces **FRESH MOZZARELLA CHEESE**, sliced into ⅛-inch rounds and patted dry

Hand-torn **FRESH BASIL LEAVES**, for garnish

RECIPE CONTINUES

Arrange the eggplant slices on 2 large baking sheets and sprinkle on both sides with a light coating of salt. Set aside to let the salt draw out the bitter juices from the eggplant, about 45 minutes. Blot and lightly press the eggplant slices with paper towels so each slice is dry, then stack on a cutting board. Wipe both baking sheets clean.

In a shallow bowl, whisk together the panko, ¼ cup of Parmesan, the oregano, granulated garlic, 1 teaspoon salt, and a couple grinds of black pepper. In a second shallow bowl, stir together the flour and a pinch of salt and pepper. In a third shallow bowl, whisk together the eggs, a splash of water, and a large pinch of salt and pepper.

Working in small batches, dredge the eggplant slices first in the flour, then coat in the beaten egg, and then dredge in the panko mixture. Shake off excess breading and transfer the breaded eggplant to one of the baking sheets.

Fill a large, deep cast-iron skillet halfway with oil and heat to 375°F over medium-high

heat. Place a wire rack on the second baking sheet. Pour the marinara sauce into a medium saucepan and bring to a simmer over medium heat, 6 to 8 minutes, stirring occasionally. Turn off the heat and cover with a lid to keep warm.

Working in small batches, fry the eggplant slices, turning once, until the breading is golden brown and crispy and the centers are tender (almost creamy in texture), about 2 minutes per side. Transfer the fried eggplant to the wire rack.

Preheat the oven to 400°F.

In a medium bowl, combine the ricotta, goat cheese, and cream. Season with salt and pepper, and whisk until smooth. Stir in the parsley.

Cover the bottom of a 9 by 13-inch baking dish with 1 cup of the marinara sauce and arrange half the fried eggplant on the sauce (some overlap is fine). Cover the eggplant with the ricotta cheese mixture, then top with 1½ cups of the marinara sauce. Layer half the mozzarella slices over the sauced eggplant and sprinkle with half the remaining Parmesan. Repeat with the remaining eggplant, marinara sauce, mozzarella, and Parmesan cheese. Place the baking dish on a large baking sheet and bake until the mozzarella is melted and browned in spots, about 30 minutes, rotating the baking sheet once after 15 minutes.

Rest the baked eggplant for 15 minutes. Garnish with the basil leaves, cut into individual pieces, and serve.

Queen's Tip

Combine these recipes to make a dinner fit for the Governor!
Radish Salad (page 102)
Eggplant Parmesan (page 161)
Ginger Ale (page 52)
Banana Pudding (page 86)

GUS'S FAMOUS MARINARA SAUCE

Makes about 4 cups

1 (28-oz) can whole peeled San Marzano plum tomatoes in puree

3 tablespoons extra-virgin olive oil

1 small yellow onion, finely chopped

Kosher salt

3 garlic cloves, minced

1 (15-oz) can crushed tomatoes

¼ teaspoon red pepper flakes

¾ teaspoon dried oregano

1 bay leaf

⅓ cup lightly packed fresh basil leaves

Put the plum tomatoes (and puree) in a large bowl. Use your hands to crush the tomatoes into bite-size pieces.

In a small Dutch oven set over medium heat, warm the olive oil. Add the onion, season with salt, and cook, stirring occasionally, until tender, 10 to 12 minutes. Add the garlic and cook, stirring constantly, until softened, 1 to 2 minutes. Add the hand-crushed tomatoes, the canned tomatoes, red pepper flakes, oregano, and bay leaf. Season lightly with salt and cook, stirring occasionally, until the sauce starts to lightly bubble, about 5 minutes. Partially cover the Dutch oven with a lid and continue to simmer the sauce until reduced by about one-third and thickened, about 1 hour, stirring occasionally.

Discard the bay leaf. Add the basil and stir until wilted. Season the sauce with additional salt, if needed. Use immediately or cool completely and then transfer to an airtight container and refrigerate for up to 5 days or freeze for up to 6 months.

"Ever since I was a little girl, I've always gotten a kick out of the way the cheese stretches as you lift each serving out of the baking dish. I think that's half the reason I love Eggplant Parmesan so much; it's as fun to serve and eat as it is tasty!" -JODI

Baked Fish

FROM THE KITCHEN OF:	THE QUEEN OF SAUCE	YIELD: MAKES 2 TO 4 SERVINGS

We're going to prepare a bevy of succulent whole fish, lightly floured and seasoned and quickly crisped on the stovetop. Then we'll crank up the seasonings and roast the fish in the oven. For the finishing touch, we'll plate them on a bed of fresh herbs and even more lemon slices; the aroma alone is entrancing!

We'll be using trout in our recipe, but feel free to sub any similar fish, depending on what's available to you. You can serve each person a whole fish if you like, or split each fish between two guests. It all depends on the size of the fish, as well as the size of everyone's appetite. But I think one small fish per plate achieves the best visual appeal. Baked Fish pairs beautifully with Fiddlehead Risotto; their savory aromas are a perfect match that will have everyone coming back for more!

INGREDIENTS

1 large bunch **FRESH LEMON THYME** (about ¾ oz)

1 large bunch **FRESH OREGANO** (about ¾ oz)

8 **FRESH BAY LEAVES**

⅓ cup **ALL-PURPOSE FLOUR**

⅓ cup **CORNSTARCH**

2 (1 to 1¼ lb) whole **RAINBOW TROUT**, cleaned (see Queen's Tip)

KOSHER SALT and **FRESHLY GROUND BLACK PEPPER**

NEUTRAL HIGH-HEAT COOKING OIL, TALLOW, or **LARD,** for shallow-frying

1 large bunch **FRESH DILL** (about 2 oz), stems trimmed

1 large bunch **FRESH FLAT-LEAF PARSLEY** (about 3 oz), stems trimmed

4 **GARLIC CLOVES**, thinly sliced

2 small **LEMONS**, 1 thinly sliced into rounds and 1 cut into wedges

Queen's Tip

If the fish are a little too large for the skillet you are using, remove the tails to make them fit.

"This reminds me of the sorts of meals we enjoyed at the Grampleton River dig site back in the day; we actually made a little clay oven to bake fish from the river. That crispy skin and juicy, flaky meat were just the inspiration we needed to keep digging all night by lanternlight." **-GUNTHER**

Preheat the oven to 400°F. Fit a wire rack in a rimmed baking sheet.

On the rack, arrange the lemon thyme, oregano, and bay leaves in 2 long piles that are about the length and width of the trout.

In a small bowl, combine the flour and cornstarch, then spread the mixture evenly across a small baking dish or sheet. Season the fish liberally inside and out with salt and pepper. Then, one at a time, dredge each fish evenly in the flour mixture.

Place an extra-large cast-iron skillet on medium-high heat, and pour in enough oil to cover the bottom of the skillet by ¼ inch. The oil is hot enough when you sprinkle in a small pinch of the flour mixture and it immediately sizzles. Pick up one of the fish by the tail and shake off any excess flour. Carefully lay the fish in the hot oil and cook until the skin is lightly browned and crispy, about 2 minutes. Use a large metal spatula and tongs to carefully turn the fish over and cook on the other side until the skin is again lightly browned and crispy (the fish will not be cooked through at this point), about 2 minutes. Transfer the fish onto one of the piles of herbs. Repeat to fry the second trout, again placing it on the other pile of herbs on the rack.

Use the rounded backside of a spoon to carefully lift open the fish and fill the inside with one-fourth of the dill, one-fourth of the parsley, half the garlic slices, and half the lemon slices. Place in the oven on the rack and bake the fish until flaky, about 15 minutes.

Meanwhile, on 2 large oval plates, arrange a bed of the remaining dill and parsley. Place a baked fish on top of the herbs on each plate, arrange the lemon wedges around the fish, and serve immediately.

Queen's Tip

If you're looking for some recipes to celebrate Feast of the Winter Star, look no further! Start with an appetizer of Pepper Poppers (page 158), add the Roots Platter (page 146) and Baked Fish for dinner, and end the meal with a slice of Chocolate Cake (page 178) and a Triple Shot Espresso (page 182).

Baked Fish
164

Seafoam
Pudding
168

Seafoam Pudding

SQUID INK CONGEE TOPPED WITH MARINATED FISH

FROM THE KITCHEN OF: THE QUEEN OF SAUCE

YIELD: MAKES 4 TO 6 SERVINGS

I imagine a crew of pirates, sailing the ocean for weeks on end with bags upon bags of rice in the ship's larder and all the fish they could ever want. Not content with the same meal over and over again, the cook decides to get creative. Carp and flounder fillets are marinated in soy sauce and sesame oil with ginger, garlic, and white pepper. Meanwhile, fluffy rice is slowly cooked in a bath of umami-rich fish broth. Combine the two, and voilà! The entire crew gets to enjoy a savory, filling rice porridge loaded with that flavorful fish. I officially dub this dish Seafoam Pudding!

There's no need to be jealous of that hypothetical pirate crew; we can enjoy that very same maritime delicacy here on dry land! We'll even take it a step further by adding squid ink for extra flavor and a mysterious splash of color. But don't be discouraged if you can't get ahold of any squid ink (it is sold in jars); this is a delicious dish with or without it. Ahoy, landlubbers, culinary adventures await!

INGREDIENTS

1 (4-inch) piece **FRESH GINGER**

2 **GARLIC CLOVES**

3 tablespoons **SOY SAUCE**, plus more for serving

1 tablespoon **TOASTED SESAME OIL**, plus more as needed

1 teaspoon **GROUND WHITE PEPPER**, plus more for serving

12 ounces **FLOUNDER FILLETS**, cut into 2-inch (5 cm) pieces

12 ounces **CARP** (or **COD**) fillets, skin removed, cut into 2-inch pieces

1 cup **JASMINE RICE**

2 quarts good-quality **FISH STOCK**

2 cups **WATER**

2 to 3 teaspoons **SQUID INK** (optional)

½ cup thinly sliced **SCALLIONS** (white and green parts)

½ cup coarsely chopped **FRESH CILANTRO LEAVES** and soft stems

Queen's Tip
If you can't find carp or flounder, cod makes an excellent alternative.

Use tongs to lift the fish pieces, one by one, from the marinade (discard the marinade) and gently nestle them in the simmering rice pudding. Cover with a lid and simmer until the fish is just cooked through and becoming flaky, about 10 minutes, lifting the lid and gently stirring occasionally (if some of the fish breaks apart, that is okay). The pudding will be thick, but you can stir in additional hot water (or stock) to make it thinner, if you prefer.

To serve, ladle the seafoam pudding into individual bowls, then drizzle with additional sesame oil and sprinkle with additional white pepper, if desired. Top with the sliced ginger, the scallions, and cilantro. Serve immediately, with additional soy sauce on the side.

Peel the ginger and cut in half. Finely grate half the ginger on a box grater and place in a medium bowl. Cut the remaining ginger into very thin matchsticks. Finely grate the garlic and add to the bowl with the ginger. Stir in the 3 tablespoons soy sauce, 1 tablespoon toasted sesame oil, and 1 teaspoon white pepper. Add the fish and gently stir until the pieces are coated with seasoning. Place in the refrigerator to chill.

Put the rice in a fine-mesh strainer and quickly rinse with cold water.

In a medium Dutch oven over medium-high heat, combine the stock, water, and rice. Bring to a boil, stirring occasionally, then reduce the heat to low and simmer, stirring occasionally, until the rice is soft and the mixture is thick and slightly creamy, about 1 hour. (The consistency will be similar to porridge or a slightly looser rice pudding.) Stir in the squid ink, if using.

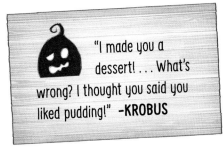

"I made you a dessert! . . . What's wrong? I thought you said you liked pudding!" -KROBUS

Spaghetti
WITH BUTTERNUT SQUASH PASTA

| FROM THE KITCHEN OF: | LEWIS | | YIELD: MAKES 6 SERVINGS |  |

Back when the community center was still up and running, we used to do a spaghetti dinner once a week. It was a good way to get everyone together and catch up on the happenings, all while enjoying big saucy bowls of spaghetti. And when I say spaghetti, I'm talking fresh homemade pasta, not the store-bought stuff.

These days, I don't think a lot of folks know how fun and rewarding it can be to make your own pasta. All you need are a few ingredients—ones I'll bet you already have at home—and a little elbow grease. You can even add butternut squash to the dough for some extra seasonal sweetness. Just make sure you roll the dough out nice and level, or else the noodles won't cook evenly.

Of course, the sauce is just as important as the noodles. I personally love using lots of chopped mushrooms for flavor and texture, along with aromatic veggies. Make sure to use the very best tomatoes you can get!

INGREDIENTS

Butternut Squash Pasta

1 small **BUTTERNUT SQUASH** (about 2 lb; 900 g)

2 tablespoons **EXTRA-VIRGIN OLIVE OIL**

1 **LARGE EGG**

1 **LARGE EGG YOLK**

3¼ cups (455 g) **ALL-PURPOSE FLOUR**, plus more for dusting

KOSHER SALT

Mushroom Bolognese

6 **GARLIC CLOVES**

8 ounces (225 g) **WHITE BUTTON MUSHROOMS**, coarsely chopped

8 ounces (225 g) **FRESH CREMINI MUSHROOMS**, coarsely chopped

2 small **CELERY STALKS**, coarsely chopped

1 medium **CARROT**, peeled and coarsely chopped

1 medium **YELLOW ONION**, coarsely chopped

5 tablespoons (75 ml) **EXTRA-VIRGIN OLIVE OIL**

KOSHER SALT

½ teaspoon **RED PEPPER FLAKES**

2 teaspoons chopped **FRESH OREGANO LEAVES**, or 1 teaspoon **DRIED OREGANO**

⅓ cup (85 g) **TOMATO PASTE**

⅔ cup (160 ml) **DRY RED WINE**

1 (28-oz; 794 g) can **CRUSHED PEELED TOMATOES IN PUREE**

⅓ cup (80 ml) **WHOLE MILK**

2 tablespoons **UNSALTED BUTTER**

Serving

Freshly grated **PARMESAN CHEESE**

Hand-torn **FRESH BASIL LEAVES**

EXTRA-VIRGIN OLIVE OIL

FOR THE PASTA: Preheat the oven to 375°F (190°C). Line a baking sheet with parchment paper.

Carefully cut the butternut squash in half, use a spoon to remove the seeds from the center, and scrape out as many of the strings as possible. Use your hands to liberally rub water all over the inside and the outside of the squash halves, then place cut side down on the baking sheet. Roast until the squash is very tender (a fork should go through the skin and flesh without any effort), about 1 hour, rotating the baking sheet once after 30 minutes. Turn the squash halves cut side up and let cool completely.

Scoop the flesh of the squash into a food processor and blend until very smooth. Measure out 1¼ cups (275 g) and place in a medium bowl. (Reserve any remaining puree for another use.)

To the bowl with the squash add the olive oil, egg, and egg yolk and whisk to combine. In a large bowl, combine the 3¼ cups (455 g) flour and 1½ teaspoons of salt and use your hands to make a well in the middle of the flour. Pour the squash puree into the center and stir with a wooden spoon or rubber spatula until you have a shaggy dough. Switch to your hands and mix until you have a rough dough.

Turn out the dough onto a floured work surface and knead until the dough is smooth and supple, 6 to 8 minutes. Cover the dough with a damp kitchen towel and rest for 30 minutes at room temperature. Wrap the dough in plastic wrap and chill in the refrigerator for at least 2 hours and up to overnight.

FOR THE MUSHROOM BOLOGNESE: Put the garlic in a food processor and pulse until chopped, then transfer to a small bowl. Put the mushrooms (in batches, if needed) in the food processor and pulse until finely chopped (but not pureed). Transfer to a medium bowl. Put the celery, carrot, and onion in the food processor and pulse until chopped; leave in the food processor.

Heat 3 tablespoons of the olive oil in a large Dutch oven on medium heat. Add the chopped mushrooms and cook, stirring occasionally, until deeply browned and caramelized in spots, about 30 minutes. Scoop the mushrooms back into their bowl. Add 2 more tablespoons of olive oil and add the celery mixture from the processor, season liberally with salt, and cook, stirring occasionally, until tender and lightly caramelized, 20 to 25 minutes.

Return the mushrooms to the Dutch oven and stir to combine with the other vegetables. Add the garlic, red pepper flakes, and oregano and cook, stirring constantly, until softened, 2 to 3 minutes. Stir in the tomato paste and cook, stirring frequently, until the paste deepens in color and starts sticking to the bottom of the pot, about 5 minutes. Stir in the wine and cook, stirring frequently, for 5 minutes. Reduce the heat to medium, stir in the canned tomatoes and milk, and bring to a simmer, 7 to 10 minutes. Partially cover the Dutch oven with a lid and cook, stirring occasionally, until the sauce is reduced slightly, thickened, and robust and flavorful, about 1 hour. Stir the butter into the sauce.

TO MAKE THE PASTA: When the dough is ready, dust a baking sheet lightly with flour. Divide the chilled dough into 8 equal pieces. Lightly dust a clean, flat work surface with flour. Place one of the dough pieces (keep the other pieces on a large plate covered loosely with plastic wrap or a damp kitchen towel in the refrigerator) on the work surface and use your hands to shape it into a rectangle. Use a lightly floured rolling pin to roll the dough until it is very thin (about 1/16 inch; 2 mm). Lightly flour the top of the pasta sheet, then fold in thirds, like a letter. Lightly flour a sharp knife and cut the pasta crosswise into strands 1/4 inch (6 mm) thick.

Transfer the cut pasta in a clustered bundle to the baking sheet, making a mound, and sprinkle with flour (this keeps the pasta strands from sticking together). Repeat with the remaining 7 pasta dough pieces, making 6 even mounds by combining strands accordingly. (You are rolling out and cutting 8 pasta sheets but dividing the pasta into 6 servings.) Alternatively, you can use a pasta machine to roll and cut the pasta strands.

If you are not cooking the pasta right away, cover it loosely with plastic wrap and keep chilled in the refrigerator for up to 4 hours. If you are ready to cook the pasta, you can proceed without any chilling.

TO COOK THE PASTA: Bring a large pot of salted water to a boil over medium-high heat. Use your hands to add 1 to 2 pasta mounds to the boiling water and use tongs to gently separate the strands. Let the pasta cook undisturbed until it floats to the surface, about 1 minute, then continue to cook until it is just tender with a slight chew to it, 30 seconds to 1 minute more. Use a large spider or slotted spoon to transfer the cooked pasta to a serving bowl or plate. Repeat with the remaining pasta mounds. Reserve 1 cup (240 ml) of the pasta water; you can use it to adjust the Bolognese to the desired consistency just before serving.

SERVE THE PASTA: Reheat the sauce, if necessary, and thin if desired with the pasta water. Spoon the sauce over the pasta in the serving bowls and top with the grated cheese and the basil leaves. Drizzle with a touch of additional olive oil, if desired, and serve immediately.

Cookie

OATMEAL CHOCOLATE CHIP

FROM THE KITCHEN OF: EVELYN

YIELD: MAKES ABOUT 16 COOKIES

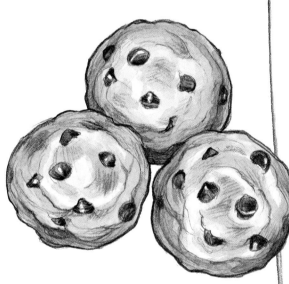

I learned this recipe from my mother when I was very young, and she learned it from her mother. And just between you and me, I may have made a few improvements! The secret is in the homemade oat flour; it adds a little something extra to the flavor and texture that you'll never find in those store-bought cookies.

I love bringing a batch of piping hot cookies fresh from the oven as a housewarming gift; even if it's not a special occasion, I like to bake a batch or two every now and then, just in case an unexpected visitor drops by!

INGREDIENTS

¾ cup (1½ sticks; 165 g) **UNSALTED BUTTER**

¾ cup (70 g) quick-cooking **OATS**

1 cup (140 g) **ALL-PURPOSE FLOUR**

1 teaspoon **BAKING SODA**

KOSHER SALT

¾ cup (150 g) firmly packed **LIGHT BROWN SUGAR**

½ cup (100 g) **GRANULATED SUGAR**

1 **LARGE EGG** plus 1 **EGG YOLK**, at room temperature

2 teaspoons **VANILLA EXTRACT**

1¼ cups (225 g) **SEMISWEET CHOCOLATE CHIPS**

In a medium saucepan over medium heat, melt the butter. Continue to cook, stirring frequently, until light brown specks start to form and the butter starts to smell nutty, 7 to 10 minutes. Pour the butter and any browned bits into a large bowl and set aside to cool slightly, about 30 minutes, stirring occasionally.

Add the oats to a blender and blend until finely ground. Transfer to a medium bowl and add the flour, baking soda, and ¾ teaspoon salt. Whisk to combine.

To the slightly cooled browned butter (it should no longer be hot to the touch, but it is okay if it is still a tad warm), add the brown sugar and granulated sugar. Whisk until smooth. Add the egg, egg yolk, and vanilla and whisk again until smooth. Add the oat-flour mixture and use a rubber spatula to stir until just combined. Fold in the chocolate chips.

Cover the bowl and refrigerate the dough until firm enough to easily scoop, about 30 minutes. (See Queen's Tip.)

"I do love the scent of fresh-baked cookies; It makes the customers hungry, too, so they end up buying a little more of everything. Hmm . . . Maybe I can convince Abigail to take up daily cookie-baking as a hobby . . ." –PIERRE

Line a small baking sheet with parchment paper or a silicone mat. Divide the dough into 3-tablespoon (55 g) mounds (about 16 cookies total) and place on the baking sheet. Cover the dough and chill in the refrigerator until completely firm, at least 1 hour and up to 48 hours.

When you are ready to bake, preheat the oven to 350°F (175°C) and line 2 large baking sheets with parchment paper.

Transfer 6 portions of the cookie dough onto one of the baking sheets, spacing them evenly apart (the cookies spread quite a bit as they bake). Place the baking sheet in the oven and bake until the cookie edges are set and lightly browned and the centers are lightly puffed but still soft (the center of the cookies might seem underbaked, but that is okay; the cookies will collapse slightly and set up fully as they cool), 12 to 14 minutes, rotating the baking sheet once halfway through the baking time.

While the first sheet is baking, place 6 portions on the second baking sheet. Remove the first baking sheet from the oven and let the cookies cool for 5 minutes, then transfer them to a wire rack to cool completely. Place the second sheet in the oven and repeat the baking and cooling process. While the second sheet is baking, add the remaining 4 portions on the first baking sheet, now cooled. When the second sheet comes out of the oven, replace it with the final batch of cookies and bake and cool as before.

Queen's Tip

For freshly baked cookies at a moment's notice, you can portion and freeze the cookie dough on a baking sheet lined with parchment paper or a silicone mat. Once frozen, transfer the cookie portions to an airtight container or storage bag and store in the freezer for up to 3 months. Then place the frozen cookie dough on a baking sheet and put in a preheated oven, allowing 2 to 3 minutes additional baking time.

Poppyseed Muffin

FROM THE KITCHEN OF: **THE QUEEN OF SAUCE**

YIELD: **MAKES 12 MUFFINS**

Though plenty of flavors pair well with the nutty crunch of poppy seeds, no flavor goes hand in hand more naturally with them than lemon. There's a reason why so many poppyseed muffin recipes call for this pairing, and I say if it ain't broke, don't fix it! We'll throw in some buttermilk for a bit of additional tanginess and to produce a texture so soft and fluffy you might accidentally mistake it for your favorite pillow. Talk about sweet dreams! Be careful not to put too much batter in each cup; the muffins expand while baking, and we don't want to go ruining that perfect little muffin shape by having them overflow!

INGREDIENTS

2 cups (280 g) **ALL-PURPOSE FLOUR**

2 tablespoons plus 1 teaspoon **POPPY SEEDS**

2 teaspoons **BAKING POWDER**

KOSHER SALT

¼ teaspoon **BAKING SODA**

1 cup (200 g) **GRANULATED SUGAR**

1 tablespoon grated **FRESH LEMON ZEST**

¾ cup (175 ml) **BUTTERMILK**, at room temperature

2 **LARGE EGGS**, at room temperature

2 tablespoons **EXTRA-VIRGIN OLIVE OIL**

2 tablespoons **FRESH LEMON JUICE**

2 teaspoons pure **VANILLA EXTRACT**

6 tablespoons (90 g) **UNSALTED BUTTER**, melted and cooled slightly

2 tablespoons **RAW** or **TURBINADO SUGAR**

After 20 minutes, preheat the oven to 400°F (200°C).

Divide the batter evenly among the cups in the muffin tin (about a heaping ¼ cup batter per cup). Do not flatten the batter; leave it in fluffy mounds. Sprinkle the tops with the raw or turbinado sugar. Bake the muffins for 10 minutes, then reduce the temperature to 375°F (190°C) and continue to bake until the tops and edges of the muffins are light golden brown and a cake tester or toothpick inserted into a muffin center comes out clean, 10 to 12 additional minutes.

Cool the muffins in the tin for 5 minutes, then transfer to a wire rack to cool completely before serving.

Line a standard 12-cup muffin tin with cupcake liners (preferably in the color purple).

In a large bowl, whisk together the flour, poppy seeds, baking powder, ½ teaspoon salt, and the baking soda.

In a medium bowl, combine the granulated sugar and lemon zest and use your fingers to rub them together until the mixture has the texture of wet sand. Add the buttermilk, eggs, olive oil, lemon juice, and vanilla. Whisk until smooth, then slowly whisk in the melted butter until well combined.

Pour the buttermilk mixture into the dry ingredients and use a rubber spatula to gently stir until the batter is just combined (a few lumps are fine). Do not overmix. Set the batter aside to rest for 30 minutes at room temperature. The batter will become slightly fluffy during this time and will ensure a domed muffin with a light crumb.

"I don't come across poppies very often while foraging, but Evelyn lets me harvest seeds from the ones in the town garden every year. Lucky for me, I can get enough seeds for a whole batch of muffins from just a few flowers!" –LEAH

Chocolate Cake

FROM THE KITCHEN OF: THE QUEEN OF SAUCE

YIELD: MAKES 24 TO 36 SERVINGS

I don't mean to boast, but as far as desserts go, I don't think there's anything better known and better loved than my classic chocolate cake. It's chocolate all the way through, with a rich, creamy ganache frosting nestled between velvety layers of cake. But why stop there? Adding chocolate chips to each layer of frosting creates fun texture variations in each bite, and a sprinkling of even more chocolate chips on the outside of the finished cake gives it that extra visual something. And of course, the finishing touch had to be a literal cherry on top.

We'll also add a generous amount of strong coffee to the batter—our Triple Shot Espresso, for example—to give the cake an exotic depth of flavor that will take it to the next level. It may sound odd, but coffee actually enhances the chocolate flavor!

INGREDIENTS

Chocolate Cake

2 cups (4 sticks; 440 g) **UNSALTED BUTTER,** plus more for greasing

2 cups (160 g) **UNSWEETENED COCOA POWDER,** plus more for dusting

2 cups (475 ml) strong **COFFEE**

4½ cups (630 g) **ALL-PURPOSE FLOUR**

2 teaspoons **BAKING POWDER**

2 teaspoons **BAKING SODA**

1½ teaspoons **KOSHER SALT**

3 cups (600 g) firmly packed **DARK BROWN SUGAR**

2 cups (480 g) **SOUR CREAM,** at room temperature

½ cup (120 ml) **EXTRA-VIRGIN OLIVE OIL**

1 tablespoon **PURE VANILLA EXTRACT**

6 **LARGE EGGS,** at room temperature

Chocolate Ganache Frosting

1¼ pounds (570 g) good-quality **BITTERSWEET CHOCOLATE,** finely chopped

2¼ cups (530 ml) **HEAVY CREAM**

KOSHER SALT

¾ cup (90 g) **CONFECTIONERS' SUGAR**

Assembly

2 cups (360 g) **SEMISWEET CHOCOLATE CHIPS,** plus more for sprinkling

1 **MARASCHINO CHERRY,** stem removed, patted dry

Special Equipment

3 **CAKE PANS:** 10-inch (25 cm) round, 8-inch (20 cm) round, and 5-inch (13 cm) round

FOR THE CAKE LAYERS: Generously grease a 10-inch (25 cm), 8-inch (20 cm), and 5-inch (13 cm) round cake pan with butter, then evenly dust with cocoa powder. Shake out any excess cocoa, then line each pan with a round of parchment paper. Lightly grease the parchment paper with more butter.

In a medium saucepan over medium heat, combine the 2 cups (440 g) butter and 2 cups (475 ml) coffee. Cook, stirring occasionally, until the butter is melted and the mixture comes to a simmer, 10 to 15 minutes. Remove from the heat, add the 2 cups (160 g) cocoa powder, and whisk until smooth. Let cool for 30 minutes, whisking occasionally. (It is ready to use when barely warm to the touch; as it cools, the mixture might start to look separated, and that is okay.)

Preheat the oven to 350°F (175°C).

Place a fine-mesh strainer over a medium bowl, then sift the flour, baking powder, and baking soda into the bowl. Add the salt and whisk to combine.

In an extra-large bowl, whisk together the brown sugar, sour cream, olive oil, and vanilla until smooth. Whisk in the eggs, one at a time, whisking well after each addition. In 3 additions, whisk in one-third of the flour with half the cocoa mixture (give it a good whisk before adding to the flour mixture), then another one-third of the flour with the remaining cocoa mixture; lastly, add the remaining flour. Whisk until the batter is smooth.

Scoop 1½ cups (260 g) of the batter into the small pan, 4 cups (960 g) into the medium pan, and the remaining batter into the large pan. Smooth the tops, then lightly drop each pan on a flat surface several times to help further settle the batter and remove air bubbles.

Depending on the size of your oven, you can bake the cakes on the same rack or on 2 racks in the upper and lower thirds of the oven. Bake until the tops are puffed and a cake tester inserted into the center comes out clean, about 35 minutes for the small pan, 50 minutes for the medium pan, and 1 hour for the large pan. After removing the small cake from the oven, rotate the 2 larger ones front to back. (The tops of the cakes might crack as they bake, and that is okay.)

Transfer the cakes to a wire rack and let cool for 15 minutes in the pan. After 15 minutes, carefully invert each cake onto the wire rack, remove the parchment paper, and let cool completely.

Once the cakes are cool, use a serrated knife to trim the tops of the cake so they are flat. Use the knife to slice each cake in half to create two even layers out of each cake. Loosely cover the cakes.

FOR THE FROSTING: Place the chocolate in a large bowl. In a small saucepan over medium heat, warm the cream, stirring occasionally, until it just starts to simmer, 10 to 15 minutes.

Pour the hot cream over the chocolate, gently shake the bowl so that the chocolate is submerged in the cream, and let sit for 5 minutes. Gently stir until the chocolate is completely melted and the ganache is smooth. Stir in ½ teaspoon salt, then let cool completely, about 1 hour, stirring occasionally. Then refrigerate, stirring well every 5 minutes, until it is between a thick pudding and a fudgy frosting, 15 to 30 minutes.

Sift the confectioners' sugar over the ganache and use a whisk to blend until smooth. Place the frosting in the refrigerator for 5 minutes. (This final chill gives the sugar some time to thicken the mixture so it will be sturdy between the layers of cake.) The frosting is ready when it turns from semi-glossy to matte.

ASSEMBLE THE CAKE: Spread a couple small spoonfuls of the frosting in the center of an extra-large cake stand or platter, then place one of the large layers cut side up on the

frosting (this helps keep the cake in place while you stack it). Spread 1⅓ cups (305 g) of frosting on the top of the cake, then sprinkle evenly with 1 cup (180 g) of chocolate chips. Stack the second large layer cut side down on top of the chocolate chips. Frost the top with another 1⅓ cups (305 g) frosting.

Stack a medium cake layer cut side up on top of the last layer and spread ¾ cup (170 g) of frosting on top, then sprinkle evenly with ¾ cup (135 g) chocolate chips. Stack the second medium layer cut side down on top of the chocolate chips. Frost the top with another ¾ cup (170 g) frosting.

Stack a small layer on top of the last one and spread ½ cup (115 g) of frosting on top, then sprinkle evenly with ¼ cup (45 g) chocolate chips. Stack the last layer cut side down on top of the chocolate chips. Frost the top of the cake with the remaining frosting. Sprinkle additional chocolate chips on top. Place the maraschino cherry in the center and serve.

"I can never seem to find the right occasion for a chocolate cake; Vincent prefers fruity flavors, and Sam would rather have a maple bar. And of course Kent's never really been into sweets. Maybe I'll see if Kent and the boys can handle making one for me on my birthday." **–JODI**

Triple Shot Espresso

SPICED COFFEE CONCENTRATE

| FROM THE KITCHEN OF: | GUS | | YIELD: | MAKES ABOUT 2⅔ CUPS OF CONCENTRATE |

Ah, the joy of that first cup of coffee in the morning, that third cup with lunch, that fifth cup after dinner . . . well, let's not get carried away! There are countless ways to prepare a cup of coffee. For those of you with fancy espresso machines, sure, you can just pull yourself a triple shot and call it a day. But with some time and patience, and a simple coffee grinder, we can make ourselves a strong, tasty coffee concentrate without any expensive equipment at all. And as an added bonus, we'll be able to infuse our concentrate with spices and other wonderful flavors.

INGREDIENTS

2 **CINNAMON STICKS**

3 **GREEN CARDAMOM PODS**

4 whole **CLOVES**

2 cups **DARK-ROAST ESPRESSO BEANS** (about 4½ oz)

4 cups cold filtered **WATER**

Use your hands to crack the cinnamon sticks in half. Add them to a coffee or spice grinder along with the cardamom pods and cloves. Pulse several times to break up the spices into smaller pieces but not until finely ground. Transfer the spices to a half-gallon container. In batches, grind the espresso beans in a coffee grinder to a medium-fine grind (the texture should be similar to coarse kosher salt) and add to the container with the spices. Add the water and stir until well combined.

Cover the container, transfer to the refrigerator, and let steep for at least 18 and up to 24 hours. (The longer you steep the coffee, the stronger the concentrate will be.)

Line a large fine-mesh strainer with a large coffee filter and place the strainer over a large bowl. Pour the steeped coffee grounds and all the liquid into the coffee filter and allow it to slowly strain. Discard the coffee grounds. Transfer the espresso concentrate to a large glass bottle or jar with a lid. Store in the refrigerator for up to 14 days.

Queen's Tip

Enjoy the espresso concentrate as a chilled single, double, or triple shot of espresso. It can also be used to make your favorite espresso-based coffee drinks, such as lattes, mochas, or Americanos. If you prefer your espresso hot, gently heat it in a small saucepan over low heat until it is hot and steamy, but do not let it simmer or come to a boil; this might cause the espresso to become bitter.

"This stuff is the secret to my survival in the Mines; I bring a thermos full of it with me every time I head down. If I can't beat the monsters down there, I know I can outrun them, thanks to Triple Shot Espresso!" **-MARLON**

MR. QI'S CHECKLIST

Never stop striving to achieve perfection. Keep working hard, and I know someday you'll achieve excellence.

SPRING

- ❏ COMPLETE BREAKFAST 18
- ❏ FARMER'S LUNCH 22
- ❏ VEGETABLE STOCK 25
- ❏ CHOWDER 26
- ❏ FIDDLEHEAD RISOTTO 28
- ❏ PIZZA 32
- ❏ CARP SURPRISE 36
- ❏ STIR FRY 40
- ❏ CHEESE CAULIFLOWER 42
- ❏ SALAD 44
- ❏ RICE PUDDING 47
- ❏ RHUBARB PIE 49
- ❏ GINGER ALE 52

SUMMER

- ❏ BREAD AND BRUSCHETTA 58
- ❏ MAKI ROLL 64
- ❏ FRUIT SALAD 66
- ❏ TROPICAL CURRY 68
- ❏ LUCKY LUNCH 72
- ❏ SHRIMP COCKTAIL 74
- ❏ CRAB CAKES 77
- ❏ FISH TACO 80
- ❏ MANGO STICKY RICE 84
- ❏ BANANA PUDDING 86
- ❏ PINK CAKE 88
- ❏ BLUEBERRY TART 92
- ❏ PIÑA COLADA 95

FALL

WINTER

ERIC

Thanks to Amber Hageman, Carly Benhaim, Rosie Leick, and Odeline Mateu-Silvernail for their thoughtfulness and critiques.

To Susan Vu for her creativity and culinary expertise in bringing the Stardew Valley dishes to life. To Ryan Novak and Kari Fry, for imparting a heartfelt spirit of Stardew Valley into these pages through their respective writings and illustrations.

Thanks to Evi Abeler and her team for the beautiful photography. And to Matt Belford, Kimmy Tejasindhu, Ian Dingman, Patricia Shaw, Kelli Tokos, and everyone else at Penguin Random House who helped make this book happen.

Most important, to all the fans who have helped make Stardew Valley what it is today, thank you.

RYAN WOULD LIKE TO THANK

My parents, John and Debra, who always supported my geeky hobbies and distinct lack of exposure to sunlight. I miss you both.

My brother, Jason, for sharing so many of my interests, and for being so easy to talk to about anything or nothing important.

My partner, Kari, whose artwork also graces the pages of this cookbook. I wouldn't be where I am today without you.

Eric Barone and Amber Hageman, for so graciously allowing me to continue being a voice in the Stardew Valley universe.

Matt Belford and Kimmy Tejasindhu at Penguin Random House, for running such a tight ship and making this whole bookmaking process smooth and fun.

My D&D group, for lending me a chorus of friendly ears any time I need them: Jacob and Alix Pozderac, Nikki and George Wolfe, Sheila Saxer, Amanda Zisk, and Austin Schnepp.

KARI FRY WOULD LIKE TO THANK

her dad, Glen Fry, for teaching her the importance of hard work and resourcefulness, and that "it's better to be lucky than good."

CREDITS

Eric "ConcernedApe" Barone

Amber Hageman

Cole Medeiros

Susan Vu

Ryan Novak

Kari Fry

Matt Belford

Kimmy Tejasindhu

Evi Abeler

Chris Tanigawa

Kelli Tokos

Patricia Shaw

Ian Dingman

Lydia Estrada

Sarah Malarkey

Laura Palese

Ashleigh Heaton

Lauren Ealy

Annie Lowell

Hannah Hunt

INDEX

Note: Page references in *italics* indicate photographs.

ERIC BARONE (ConcernedApe)

From a young age, Eric had an eclectic set of interests. These ranged from learning how computers worked (and an obsession with his family's Stanley garage door opener), to philosophy and psychology, as well as making music, writing poetry, and exploring many forms of visual art. After considering studying music or astronomy in college, he ultimately decided to pursue a computer science degree out of practicality. He thought in the meantime, he would continue his artistic and musical hobbies on the side while working a "real job." After graduating and not immediately finding a position, he decided to work on a small project to add to his résumé. Realizing that making a video game was both a fun way to practice programming, and to satisfy many of his artistic impulses, he started working on a project inspired by a game he had loved as a child called Harvest Moon. Over the years, this small project grew and grew into what is now Stardew Valley, a farming video game, beloved by many. Eric has continued to support Stardew Valley over the years, releasing new content from time to time, and he was excited for the opportunity to bring some of the dishes from the game into the real world in this cookbook.

RYAN NOVAK

Born and raised in Canton, Ohio, Ryan has been a gamer almost since he learned to walk, having cut his teeth on an Atari 2600 joystick. He graduated from the University of Akron in 2006 with a bachelor of science degree in computer science; how that factors into writing video-game-related books he's still not sure, but he is fairly certain that it does somehow. His writing credits include a number of such books, including the *Stardew Valley Guidebook* (Fangamer, 2016) and the *Hollow Knight Wanderer's Journal* (Fangamer, 2019), to name just two; he has also contributed to many others as editor, producer, or whatever the situation calls for. He still lives in northeast Ohio with his partner, Kari Fry, along with several dozen plush cats (which are far easier and cheaper to take care of than real cats).

SUSAN VU

Raised in a food-centric Vietnamese American household in Seattle, Washington, Susan has spent most of her life wondering what her next amazing meal will be. Shortly after graduating from culinary school in her early twenties, she moved to New York to chase her fever dream of working in food TV. While in the city, she spent many years working as a food stylist, recipe developer, and culinary producer at notable companies such as Food Network and BuzzFeed Tasty. With a recent move back to the West Coast, she now spends most of her days recipe developing for various private clients in her home kitchen while singing and dancing to BTS.

KARI FRY

Raised on Nintendo Power magazines and video game instruction manuals, Kari has been obsessed with video games and their supplemental art since she was in second grade. Her hobbies include traveling to Japan, cooking, painting, enjoying JRPGs, and telling every bird that she loves them.

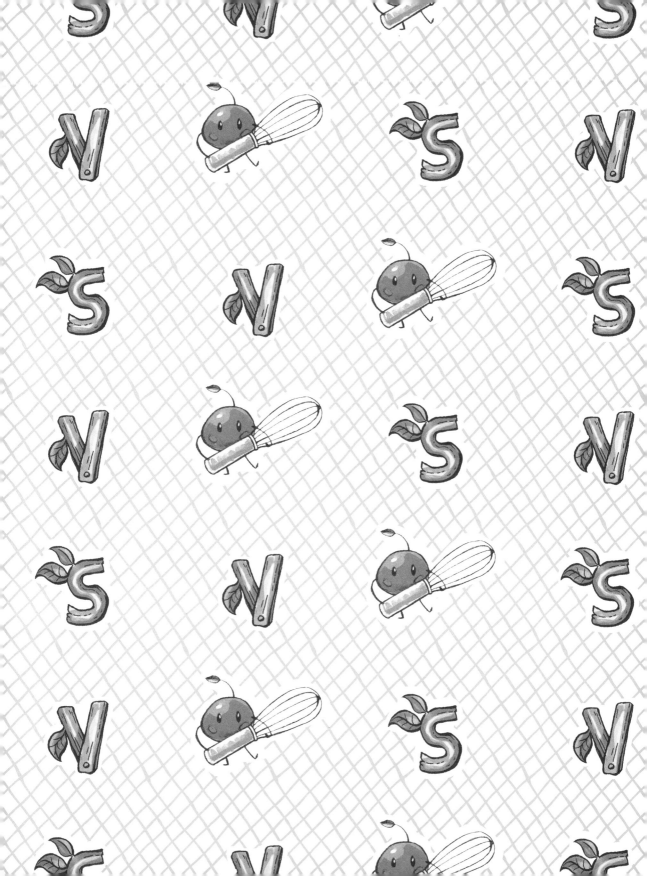